RECIPES & TALL TALES
FROM LEGENDARY RESTAURANTS OF THE Florida Keys

By Robert Stoky
Edited by Paul White

First Printing 2012
Published by Robert C. Stoky
Key Largo, Florida Keys

Printed by Central Plains Book Publishing Company

To order books contact FKRM,103900 Overseas Highway, Key Largo, FL 33037
305-451-4502

All contents copyright ©2012 Robert C. Stoky

ALL RIGHTS RESERVED. No part of this book may be reproduced or transmitted in any form, by any means, electronic or mechanical, including photocopying and recording, or by an information storage and retrieval system, except as expressly permitted in writing from the publisher. Requests for permission should be directed to Florida Keys Restaurant Management, ATTN: Permissions, 103900 Overseas Highway, Key Largo, FL, USA 33037.

ISBN 13 978-0-615-36196-3
ISBN 10 0-61536-196 X

Dedication

This book is dedicated to my father who moved his young family to the Keys in the late 1970s, to follow his dream. You not only taught us how to fish, but how to cook — literally.

To my mother for all of your love and support.

To my brother, who works side by side with me and helps to keep everything going, I could not do this without you.

To the staff members at our restaurants who serve others so that they may serve the world — you guys are amazing.

And to all of the customers who have graced the doors of one of our restaurants in the last 25 years, I am humbled by your loyalty and thank you for your business.

Keys area photos by L. Michael ("Mikey") Darden.

Mikey Darden describes himself as a "43-year-old professional house-husband," living in Deland, Florida with his wife, Adrianne.

Mikey was born and raised in Fairhope, Alabama, and it was there that he developed a love of photography and camera equipment, starting at the age of 10. What began with Mikey sneaking into his uncle's closet to play with his cameras came to fruition when he was given his own camera as a Christmas gift that year. Thus began the infatuation (he refers to it as a sickness) known as his photography hobby.

Although Mikey's work has been published, shown in a few small galleries, sold as prints, and he has occasionally been paid to shoot; he does not derive a steady income from photography and does not consider himself a 'professional' photographer. Some call him an advanced amateur or gifted hobbyist. Most call him semi-professional.

We think the photos he took for this book were outstanding! Thank you, Mikey!

Prepared food photos by Paul White.

Additional photos contributed and credited.

Ingredient photos from iStockPhoto.com

Contents

Rum Drinks & Cocktails 9
Appetizers 25
Soups, Salads & Salad Dressings 61
Entrées 83
Desserts 141
Brunch & Breakfast 157
Index 163

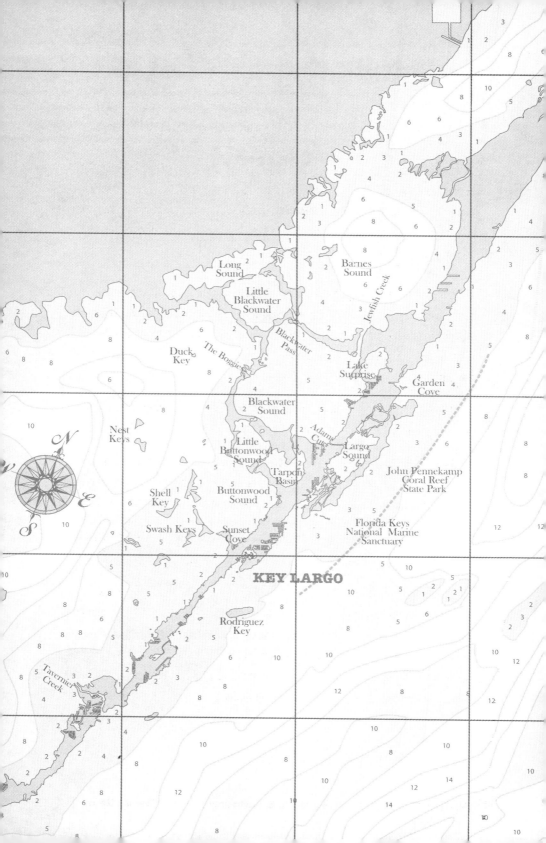

Welcome

Welcome to the Florida Keys, a 112-mile archipelago of coral and sand islands that create the southernmost place in the continental United States. As famous for our laid-back life style as we are for our amazing sunsets, the Keys are connected to the mainland by 42 bridges, and are affectionately referred to by locals as "the rock." It is not uncommon for someone to ask a local when the last time was they left the Keys, and for the local to respond that they have not been "off the rock" for over a year or more.

Inside the Florida Keys, there are five basic geographic boundaries – Key Largo, Islamorada, Marathon, Big Pine Key and the Lower Keys, and Key West. The recipes inside this book basically focus on the areas known as the Upper Keys – Key Largo, "the diving capital of the world," and Islamorada, "the fishing capital of the world."

The recipes are based on our life in the Keys. It is the food that we ate as kids — living and working off the waters of the Florida Keys.

Growing up in the Keys is different from growing up in a city like Miami. The Keys are linear, so as kids my brother Scott and I used a boat to get from Island to Island. Our boat was our car, and we went everywhere in it.

On weekdays, after school, we would often run down to our dock and head out to pull lobster traps or fish for snapper and trout in Everglades National Park.

On weekends, from sun up to sun down, we were in our boat, plying the waters off Key Largo, Tavernier, Islamorada, and Marathon. We made gas money by fishing or free diving, and then selling what we collected, and had a great time doing it. To this day, I cannot think of anything better than spending the afternoon out in the boat off Key Largo, looking at the turquoise waters, blue sky and green islands that make up the Keys –it is simply stunning. I cannot believe that we live here!

History of the Rum Runner

Holiday Isle Resort's Tiki Bar in Islamorada (now called The Postcard Inn) is the home of the World Famous Rum Runner, concocted by "Tiki" John Ebert in 1972. Made from rum, blackberry brandy, banana liqueur, grenadine, and lime juice, and served frozen, the Rum Runner packs a surprising punch. Millions of Rum Runners have been served throughout the world, and while many other bars may lay claim to creating this drink, Holiday Isle is the true birthplace of the Rum Runner. Today, the Rum Runners at Holiday Isle are made in frozen drink machines, but back in the day they were blended by hand, in a blender with ice.

The Piña Colada, always a staple of the islands, was another local favorite and it was not long before customers began asking for a drink made with half of a Rum Runner and half of a Piña Colada. Obviously, separately blending two drinks was a pain in the neck, but Tiki John never complained. He would just say, "One pain in the ass, coming up." Thus creating another Keys legend, the drink known throughout the islands of the world today as the PITA. So, the next time you are in Islamorada, make sure to try one of Tiki John's favorite frozen drinks.

The Rum Runner

Invented by "Tiki" John Ebert, in 1972, at Holiday Isle in the heart of Islamorada, this drink soon became a cherished favorite of vacationers and locals sitting at the Tiki Bar after a long day of fishing. And after a few of these, the fish stories just got a little grander.

Makes 1 drink

Ingredients:

    1 ¼ ounces Bacardi Select Rum
    ¾ ounce banana liqueur
    ¾ ounce blackberry brandy
    1 ½ ounces Giroux Grenadine
    2 ounces sour mix (if you do not have sour mix, use tart Key limeade)
    ½ ounce Bacardi 151
    a slice of orange and maraschino cherry for garnish

Preparation:

Pour all ingredients except the Bacardi 151 into a blender with ice. Mix until smooth. Pour into a tall "hurricane" glass, and top with 151. Garnish with an orange slice and a cherry.

The Piña Colada

Your search for the perfect Piña Colada is over! Pineapple plantations once ruled the land of the Florida Keys. Plantation Key is named for the pineapple plantations that were commonplace before the hurricanes of the early 1900s. You can enjoy Piña Coladas throughout the Keys, but the place that makes them best is Sundowners in Key Largo.

Makes 1 drink

Ingredients:

    2 ounces Coco Lopez cream of coconut
    2 ounces pineapple juice
    1 ¼ ounces Bacardi Silver Rum
    ½ ounce Myers's Rum
    1 tablespoon toasted flaked coconut

Preparation:

Pour all ingredients except Myers's rum into a blender with ice. Mix until smooth. Pour into a tall "hurricane" glass, and top with Myers's rum. Garnish with toasted, flaked coconut.

"Flagler's Folly"

The construction of the Overseas Railroad was a tremendous feat of engineering during the early years of the 20th century. No single construction project before or since has done more to change life in the Florida Keys.

After Henry Flagler brought the Florida East Coast Railway to Miami in the 1890s, he set his sights on Key West, to establish a deepwater port as a terminus for the railroad even closer to the newly-completed Panama Canal.

By the end of 1907, the railroad reached Knights Key, 83 miles from the mainland. The first train from the mainland arrived there in January of 1908 with regular passenger service. Knights Key served as the southern terminus of the railroad for four years.

Building a railroad in this remote part of the world was an almost impossible task. As if the heat, lack of fresh water and mosquitoes were not enough to contend with, Mother Nature threw in three hurricanes. The first, in 1906, almost brought the project to a halt. Despite 140 lives lost and losses in the millions, Flagler continued. A second storm hit in 1909. Again there was heavy damage, and 40 workers lost their lives, but Flagler was not to be deterred. When a third hurricane hit in 1910, only one life was lost.

On January 22, 1912, just a few days after his 82nd birthday, Flagler rode the first official train into Key West as bands played, whistles blew and the entire population cheered. He said, "Now I can die fulfilled." Flagler died less than 16 months later.

Already in financial trouble, the death blow to the Overseas Railroad was struck by the terrible Labor Day hurricane of 1935. More than 500 lives were lost, and most of the tracks and roadbeds in the Upper Keys were destroyed.

Because of the Depression, and because the Key West Extension had never been profitable, railroad officials decided not to rebuild. The right-of-way was sold for $640,000 to become the route for the Overseas Highway.

Flagler Express

Named after Henry Flagler's railroad, "The Railroad That Went To The Sea," this drink has been served at Marker 88 for years. A rum punch made with fresh pineapple and four flavored rums. This drink is the life of the party.

Makes 1 drink

Ingredients:
- 1 2x2 inch cube/chunk of fresh, ripe pineapple
- ½ ounce passion fruit rum
- ½ ounce orange rum
- ½ ounce coconut rum
- ½ ounce mango rum
- ¼ ounce Midori melon liqueur
- 2 ounces pineapple juice
- Slice of orange
- 1 Maraschino cherry

Preparation:
Place pineapple chunk in a glass and muddle (smash up). Add ice, rums, and pineapple juice. Stir or shake well. Garnish with a cherry and a slice of orange.

Spiced Hawaiian Punch

If you loved Hawaiian punch as a kid, then you have to try this drink. The only issue is finding the Kilo Kai spiced rum (ask your local liquor store to get this rum for you). This spiced rum is packed full of vanilla flavors and when mixed with the sweet and sour mix and the creme de noya, tastes just like your favorite youthful beverage.

Makes 1 adult beverage

Ingredients:
- ¾ ounce Kilo Kai Spiced Rum
- ¾ ounce Lazzaroni Amaretto
- ¾ ounce Triple Sec
- 1 ounce sour mix (if you do not have sour mix, use tart Key limeade)
- 1 ounce pineapple juice
- splash of Grenadine

Preparation:
Pour all ingredients except sour mix and pineapple juice into a martini shaker with ice and shake. Pour into a glass and top with sour mix and pineapple juice. Stir and enjoy!

The Mango

Mangos, native to Southeast Asia and India, are the most widely consumed fruit in the world. The mango tree can grow to over 60 feet tall, and typically fruits 2 to 4 years after planting. South Florida's warm climate is perfectly suited for the mango tree, making South Florida's mangos highly prized for their sweetness.

Simple Syrup

Makes 4 cups

Simple syrup is used to make all types of tropical drinks; so keep this on hand. It's easy to make ahead, and it keeps for days. Just keep it on the counter, unless you live in the Keys and have a sugar ant issue, then you can keep it in the refrigerator. If the sugar settles out, just reheat the entire batch!

    1 cup really hot water (almost boiling)
    3 cups sugar

Pour sugar into hot water and mix until dissolved. Store in a pitcher. Cool to room temperature.

Hemingway Cocktail

The original Daiquiri. Made just the way the Old Man drank it, back in Havana, Cuba in the 1950s. For rum drinkers, this is the drink they long for. So easy to make, yet so hard to find someone who can, or even still knows, how to make one. Of course, the recommended 28-year-old Ron Zacapa rum helps a little!

Makes 1 drink

Ingredients:

- 1 ¼ ounces 28 year old Ron Zacapa Rum
- 1 ¼ ounce simple syrup (see recipe on page 14)
- ¾ ounce fresh squeezed Key lime juice (use Persian limes if you have to)

Preparation:

Pour all ingredients into a martini shaker over ice and shake really, really hard. You want the ice chips in this drink! Strain into a short rocks glass, garnish with a lime.

21 Coconuts

A drink for rum drinkers and rum sippers. Hemingway enjoyed his rum with Key lime juice. Jimmy Buffett enjoys his favorite rum with coconut water, so in Jimmy's honor, we have included the recipe for another Marker 88 favorite, 21 Coconuts: 21 year old Zafra Rum with fresh coconut water. Amazing.

Makes 1 drink

Ingredients:

- 1 ¼ ounces 21 year old Zafra Rum
- 2 ounces fresh coconut water with a little pulp
    (or canned if you cannot get fresh)

Preparation:

Place ingredients into a martini shaker and shake hard. Pour ice and all into a short rocks glass, find your favorite palm tree, sit back, and relax. Oh yeah, listening to a little Jimmy Buffett wouldn't be a bad idea either.

Key Lime Martini

There are a couple of different versions of this drink, and all of them are good. My favorite is the one served at Sundowners in Key Largo. It's made with Keke Beach liqueur which has graham cracker flavoring, so this drink really tastes like Key lime pie. The first time I made this drink, I drank 2 pitchers, and almost forgot the recipe!

Makes 1 drink

Ingredients:

- 1 ¼ ounces citrus vodka
- 2 ounces Keke Beach liqueur
- 1 ounce pineapple juice
- ¼ ounce fresh Key lime juice (or juice from a Persian lime if you have to)
- 2 tablespoons toasted graham cracker crumbs
    (chop up graham crackers and toast)

Preparation:

Pour vodka, Keke Beach Liqueur, pineapple juice, and Key lime juice into a martini shaker with ice and shake hard. Strain and serve in a chilled martini glass with a graham cracker rim.

For the rim: Use simple syrup (see recipe on page 14) and pour on outside rim of martini glass. Then dip martini glass into toasted graham cracker crumbs to rim glass.

The Mojito

While the exact origin of this cocktail is debated, one thing is certain – Cuba is the birthplace of the mojito. Typically made of rum, it was originally thought that the lime, mint and sugar added to the drink, helped to mask the flavor of the spirit used to make the beverage.

Today, mojitos come in all flavors — watermelon, pineapple, grape, and even blueberry lime.

A classic beverage with a twist!

Sea Salt

In the Florida Keys, we are surrounded by water, so what better place to make your own sea salt? It's really easy to do, and super cool to tell your guests that you made your own!

Ingredient:

3-4 gallons of clean salt water

Preparation:

First, I like to strain my water to get out any impurities that I do not want in the final product. So I use cheese cloth and a china cap (strainer) to strain the water. If you don't have cheese cloth, then a clean t-shirt lining a strainer will do the trick. Once my water is strained, I pour it into a pot large enough to hold the water, and on the stove it goes over high heat. Allow your water to boil for 5-6 hours. Keep checking your salt, and once most of the water has evaporated, pour your salt slurry (think wet sand) into a shallow glass bowl or baking pan to dry the rest of the way. Leave the pan uncovered for a few days, stirring occasionally, until the salt has had a chance to dry completely. Store your homemade sea salt in an airtight container and use just as you would Kosher salt or other sea salts. Enjoy!

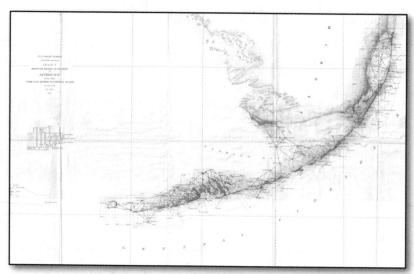
1859 US Coast Guard Survey Triangulation Map of the Florida Keys - Geographicus. Source: Wikimedia.

Watermelon Mojito

Try this summertime version of the Cuban classic. Fresh watermelon muddled with mint, limes, and rum. In Cuba, they make this drink a little stronger, with more rum, and less soda, but it packs quite a punch. This recipe has been adjusted to fit the American palate while still producing a great beverage.

Makes 1 drink

Ingredients:

1 2x2 inch cube/chunk of fresh, ripe seedless watermelon
4 large, fresh, clean mint leaves, torn in pieces
1 Key lime sliced (or ½ of a Persian lime)
1 ½ ounces Bacardi Superior Rum
1 ½ ounces simple syrup (see recipe on page 14)
2 ounces club soda

Preparation:

Place watermelon and simple syrup in a martini shaker and muddle. Add mint leaves and limes and muddle some more to release the oils in the mint and lime slices. Add ice and rum and shake hard. Pour into a tall rocks glass, add more ice if necessary, and finish with club soda. Stir and enjoy.

Classic Key Lime Mojito

Mojitos can be made with almost any type of fruit, but the granddaddy of them all is the Key Lime Mojito.

Makes 1 drink

Ingredients:

    4 large, fresh, clean mint leaves
    1 Key lime, sliced (or ½ of a Persian lime)
    1 ½ oz. Key lime rum
    1 ½ oz. simple syrup (see recipe on page 14)
    2 oz. club soda

Preparation:

In a large martini shaker add mint leaves, simple syrup, and limes and muddle to release the oils in the mint and lime slices. Add ice and rum and shake hard. Pour into a tall rocks glass, add more ice if necessary, and finish with club soda. Stir and enjoy.

Note: When making cocktails, ingredients that have bubbles, like champagne or club soda, should always be stirred in, or should top off a drink. Shaking them or stirring them too much will make the drink "flat."

Mango Mojito

South Florida is famous for super-sweet, great-tasting mangos. It's only natural, in the Keys we feature mangos in our entrées, desserts, and drinks.

Makes 1 drink

Ingredients:

    1 2x2 inch cube/chunk of fresh, ripe sweet mango
    4 large, fresh, clean mint leaves
    1 Key lime, sliced (or ½ of a Persian lime)
    1 ½ ounces Cruzan Mango Flavored Rum
    1 ½ ounces simple syrup (see recipe on page 14)
    2 ounces club soda

Preparation:

Place mango and simple syrup in a martini shaker and muddle until mango is in small chunks. Add mint leaves and limes and muddle some more to release the oils in the mint and lime slices. Add ice and rum and shake hard. Pour into a tall rocks glass, add more ice if necessary, and finish with club soda. Stir and enjoy.

The Original Margarita

Margarita Sames, a wealthy Dallas socialite, gets credit for creating the original Margarita while on vacation in Mexico during the Christmas holiday in 1948. Today, the Margarita is the most popular cocktail in the USA. The secret to her drink, as is the case for all Margaritas, is *fresh* lime juice.

Makes 1 drink

Ingredients:

2 ounces Sauza Blanco Tequila (or any tequila from Jalisco, Mexico)
1 ounce Cointreau (more flavorful and more expensive than Triple Sec)
2 fresh Key limes, juiced (add more or less to taste)
2 ounces lemon sour mix (optional)
Kosher salt and lime wedge for garnish

Preparation:

In a large martini shaker add all ingredients over ice and shake. Pour into a salt-rimmed glass.

Organic Margarita

In the last few years, organic produce and organic spirits have become very popular. This Margarita, made with organic tequila and organic agave nectar, is an amazing margarita with fewer calories, for you beachgoers, than a traditional Margarita.

Makes 1 drink

Ingredients:

1 ½ ounces Cazadores Organic Tequila
1 ounce fresh Key lime juice
¾ ounce organic agave nectar (available at your liquor or grocery store)
Kosher salt and lime wedge for garnish

Preparation:

In a large martini shaker add all ingredients over ice and shake. Pour into a salt-rimmed glass.

Coconut Margarita

Love Margaritas? Love coconut? If you do, then you're going to love these two together. Jimmy Buffett's Coconut-infused Margaritaville Tequila makes it all possible. The bartenders at Señor Frijoles in Key Largo invented this drink a few years ago, as a way to get rid of a few free bottles of tequila, and the recipe stuck. Today, it is one of their most famous cocktails.

Makes 1 drink

Ingredients:

- 1 ½ ounces Margaritaville Coconut Tequila
- ¾ ounce Cointreau
- ¾ ounce pineapple juice
- 3 ounces lemon sour mix (or really tart Key limeade)
- 2 tablespoons toasted coconut flakes

Preparation:

In a large martini shaker add all ingredients over ice and shake. Pour into a toasted coconut-rimmed margarita glass and serve.

Note: Use simple syrup (recipe on page 14) and pour on outside rim of margarita glass. Then roll the glass in toasted coconut to make a toasted coconut rim.

Grilled Pineapple Margarita

In many of the recipes inside this book, I recommend toasting, roasting, or grilling fruits and vegetables to release their flavors or to add a smoky component to a dish (or in this case, a beverage). Grilled pineapple is sweet and smoky and goes great with the oakiness of a Reposado tequila like Don Julio.

Makes 1 drink

Ingredients:

1 ripe pineapple, peel and de-core pineapple and cut into ½ inch rings
   (One pineapple should be enough for 8-10 grilled pineapple margaritas.)
1 ¼ ounces Don Julio Reposado Tequila
¾ ounce Cointreau
¾ ounce fresh Key lime juice (or fresh squeezed Persian lime juice)
3 ounces lemon sour mix
Kosher salt and lime wedge for garnish

Preparation:

Place pineapple rings on a hot barbecue grill and grill for 1-2 minutes per side. Pineapple should still be firm, but grill marks should be "set" into pineapple rings on both sides. Remove from grill, cool, dice, and refrigerate. Grilled pineapple should be prepared at least 1 hour before serving, and can be prepared up to 2 days in advance. In a large martini shaker add 2 tablespoons diced pineapple, tequila, Cointreau, Key lime juice, and sour mix. Shake hard. Serve up or on the rocks in a salted glass.

White Peach Sangria

Cool, crisp and refreshing. A delicious summertime drink. Enjoy on the boat or at the beach.

Makes 8 - 10 drinks (1 pitcher)

Ingredients:

- 2 750-ml. bottles of dry white wine (Chablis or Chardonnay)
- ¾ cup brandy
- ½ cup Triple Sec
- ¾ cup simple syrup (see recipe on page 14)
- ¾ cup peach nectar (canned is okay, or use peach puree)
- 3 oranges, sliced
- 3 green apples, cored and sliced
- 4 Key limes, sliced thin
- 4 ripe peaches, pitted and sliced

Preparation:

Combine all ingredients in a large pitcher, and refrigerate for 2 hours before serving. Serve sangria over ice.

Pomegranate Sangria

Pomegranate sangria is a little heartier than the white peach sangria above, so I recommend it for those cooler days, or for relaxing days inside, while enjoying a barbecue and the big game.

Makes 8 - 10 drinks (1 pitcher)

Ingredients:

- 2 750-ml. bottles of dry red wine (Merlot or Cabernet)
- ¾ cup brandy
- ½ cup simple syrup (see recipe on page 14)
- ¾ cup pomegranate juice
- 3 oranges, sliced
- 3 green apples, cored and sliced
- 4 Key limes, sliced thin

Preparation:

Combine all ingredients in a large pitcher, and refrigerate for 2 hours before serving. Serve sangria over ice.

History of the Conch Republic

In 1982, the United States Government installed a border control check point just south of Florida City searching for illegal immigrants and drugs being smuggled onto the "mainland" from the Florida Keys. Vehicles leaving the Keys were stopped and long traffic jams ensued.

Monroe County officials complained to the Federal government for relief, and when the complaint went unanswered, the Mayor of Key West said that if the Florida Keys were going to be treated like a foreign nation, with a border control crossing to our north, then we should become a foreign nation.

On April 23, 1982, the Florida Keys staged a mock war against the United States of America by throwing stale Cuban bread at the US Coast Guard Commander in Mallory Square in Key West, and then quickly surrendering to the commander and requesting "foreign aid." Of course the national media was on hand to record the event, and the roadblock in Florida City was quickly and quietly disbanded.

Thus was born the Conch Republic!

Our flag.

Conch Egg Rolls

The king conch is the state shell of Florida, and if you were born in the Keys you are considered a conch. In fact, the Keys themselves are known as the Conch Republic. A favorite at Marker 88 Restaurant in Islamorada, Florida, these conch egg rolls are easy to make, and are real crowd pleasers. If you cannot find ground conch, or do not like ground conch, substitute shrimp, for some quick and easy shrimp egg rolls!

Makes 10 - 12 egg rolls

Ingredients:

2 egg yolks
½ pound conch, cut into ¼ inch pieces (or substitute shrimp)
1 head Japanese cabbage (or ½ head regular cabbage if you cannot get Japanese)
1 carrot, shredded into carrot sticks
1 tablespoon Kikoman soy sauce
2 tablespoons dry white wine
¼ head of radicchio (or red cabbage)
10-12 spring roll wrappers (thinner than wonton wrappers)
1 quart vegetable oil for frying (you can fry in a pan on the stove
   or use a small home fryer at 350° F)
salt & ground white pepper to taste

Preparation:

Shred cabbage. Sauté conch with soy sauce, white wine, salt and pepper. Cook for 5 minutes, then strain and save liquid. Set conch aside to drain and cool to room temperature. Sauté cabbage and carrots in a pan with the liquid left over from cooking conch, until vegetables are coated with liquid and begin to wilt. Strain vegetables and discard liquid. Set vegetables aside, on paper towels to drain and cool to room temperature. Combine conch and vegetables and place 1½ - 2 tablespoons of mixture in the center of a spring roll wrapper, and roll into an egg roll shape. "Seal" top edge of egg roll by moistening inside top corner of the spring roll wrapper with egg yolk. Chill egg rolls for at least 30 minutes in refrigerator before frying. Fry until golden brown.

Serve with Key Lime Wasabi Aioli (see recipe on page 29).

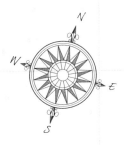

Appetizers | 27

Scott Stoky, 1978, Oceanside Marina, Key West. This 42-pound Cobia caught on 10-pound test line helped to secure the "Junior Master Angler" trophy for Stoky, the youngest Junior Master Angler ever, as part of the Metropolitan South Florida Fishing Tournament sponsored by the Miami Herald.

Key Lime Wasabi Aioli

This tangy sauce goes great with Conch Egg Rolls or Cracked Conch. Try this aioli on a grilled tuna sandwich or with fried shrimp, for added flavor with a little kick!

Makes 10 - 12 egg rolls

Ingredients:

- 5 large egg yolks, room temperature
- 6 garlic cloves, peeled and pressed
- ¼ teaspoon salt
- 2 Key limes, juiced and zested
- 1 cup vegetable oil or very light olive oil
- 4 tablespoons warm water
- ground white pepper, to taste
- 1-2 tablespoons prepared wasabi

Preparation:

Place all ingredients (except oil and wasabi) in food processor or blender and blend well. Slowly incorporate oil. Mix until aioli achieves the desired consistency. Mix in the prepared wasabi to taste. Prepare in advance, and cool in refrigerator.

Cocktail Sauce

A tangy cocktail sauce goes with any fried shellfish. Try this with Cracked Conch or peel-and-eat shrimp seasoned with Sundowners' Black Caesar's Blackening Spice.

Makes 4 servings

Ingredients:

- 6 tablespoons ketchup
- 3 tablespoons horseradish
- 4 tablespoons Key lime juice
- 2 teaspooons Tabasco sauce
- 1 teaspoon Worcestershire sauce
- salt and white pepper to taste

Preparation:

Mix well and chill. Serve when ready.

Conch Salad

A favorite in the Bahamas and the Keys. This dish is "cooked" in lime juice, like ceviche, and is served with hot sauce on the side. Enjoy this dish with fresh fried tortilla chips, or in true island style, try this with thickly sliced, fried plantain chips.

Makes 2 servings

Ingredients:

- ½ pound fresh conch, cut into ¼ inch cubes
- ¼ white onion, chopped
- 2 red tomatoes, ripe, but still firm, seeded and diced
- 1 cucumber, peeled, seeded and diced
- 1 yellow bell pepper, seeded and diced
- 1 Scotch Bonnet pepper, finely chopped
- ½ orange, peeled, seeded, and chopped
- 1 orange, juiced
- 5 Key limes, juiced (or juice of 2 Persian limes)
- salt and pepper to taste

Preparation:

Place all ingredients in a mixing bowl and mix well. Cover, refrigerate, and marinate for 3 hours. This will give the conch time to "cook" in the lime and orange juice. Serve with hot sauce on the side.

Cracked Conch

Another island favorite is Cracked Conch. Tender, battered pieces of fried conch served with dipping sauces on the side.

Makes 4 servings

Ingredients:

- 1 pound fresh conch, cut into ¼-inch thick strips
- ½ gallon coconut milk
- 2 cups of flour
- salt and pepper to taste
- 1 quart vegetable oil for frying

Preparation:

Place conch strips into coconut milk, cover, and refrigerate for at least 4 hours. Conch muscle is notoriously tough, and the coconut milk helps to tenderize the conch without adding any flavor to the conch meat. Premix flour, salt and pepper. Preheat oil to 350°. Remove conch meat from coconut milk, squeeze lightly to remove excess coconut milk and coat with flour mixture. Place conch meat into frying oil and remove when the flour has "puffed" and is a light golden color. Drain on paper towels, and serve with Key Lime Wasabi Aioli or fresh-made Cocktail Sauce (see recipes on page 29).

History of Marker 88

Founded in 1967 by Bill Baxter, Marker 88 has become a Keys' tradition. In 1967, Islamorada was much quieter than it is today, and there were only a handful of restaurants in the Islamorada area. So, after a day of charter fishing, Mr. Baxter would prepare dinner for his fishing customers. The menu was whatever they caught that day, and quickly Bill became even more famous for his cooking than he already was for his guiding abilities.

In 1978 the Baxters sold Marker 88 to Chef Andre Mueller. Andre was a classically-trained chef who spent time cooking in Europe and Hawaii before settling on the Keys. It was Andre's classical training, experiences in Hawaii, and the fruits, vegetables, and seafood of the Florida Keys that eventually led to what was considered a new type of cuisine — Floribbean — with Andre's name always mentioned as one of the pioneers of the style.

Today, Marker 88 remains one of Islamorada's premier waterfront restaurants, as we continue to recognize the legacy of the Baxters and Andre Mueller.

Conch Fritters with Curry Dipping Sauce

When visitors come to the Keys, this is the dish that they ask for the most. Conch Fritters are everyone's favorite, and in the Keys there are as many recipes for conch fritters as there are locals on the islands. This is the version that we serve at Marker 88, and we serve them with the Curry Dipping Sauce below.

Makes 8 servings

Ingredients:

1 pound fresh conch, diced into ¼-inch thick cubes
½ yellow bell pepper, diced
½ medium onion, diced
½ cup of milk
1 large garlic clove, chopped
1 egg
1 teaspoon Key lime juice
¾ cup all-purpose flour
1 tablespoon baking powder
½ tablespoon Tabasco hot sauce
½ tablespoon salt
½ teaspoon black pepper
1 quart vegetable oil for frying

Preparation:

Heat the oil in a large pot or deep fryer to 325° F. In a bowl, mix the conch, bell pepper, onion, milk, garlic, egg, Key lime juice, flour, baking powder, Tabasco, salt, and black pepper. Drop the batter by rounded tablespoons into the hot oil and fry until golden brown. Drain on paper towels. Serve with fresh Key limes and Curry Dipping Sauce.

Curry Dipping Sauce

Try this curry sauce with conch fritters, cracked conch, or with fried shrimp.

Makes 4 servings

Ingredients:

8 tablespoons mayonnaise
3 tablespoons ketchup
3 tablespoons curry powder
2 tablespoons Key lime juice

Preparation:

Mix well and refrigerate for at least 1 hour before serving.

Yellowtail Snapper Ceviche

Yellowtail snapper are plentiful off of the Keys. As long as yellowtail are caught using a size limit, and on hook and line, they are considered to be a sustainable fishery in the Keys, meaning they can be fished for, and caught, without the fishery showing any major signs of depletion. This light snapper makes a great ceviche, but if you cannot get yellowtail, any sushi-grade light white fish, like mahi mahi or grouper, will do the trick.

Makes 4 servings

Ingredients:

1 ¼ pounds fresh yellowtail snapper, cut into ½ inch cubes
5-6 garlic cloves, chopped
1 tablespoon fresh chopped cilantro
1 habanero pepper, seeded and chopped
10-12 Key limes, juiced and strained to remove pulp (or 5-6 Persian limes)
1 medium red onion, sliced thinly and rinsed
salt and ground white pepper to taste
1 ripe avocado, sliced just before serving

Preparation:

Combine all ingredients, except onion, and mix well. Lime juice should completely cover fish. Place onion slices on top of mixture and refrigerate for 2-3 hours. Before serving, mix well. Garnish with fresh avocados and serve with tortilla chips or plantain chips.

Note: A hand-press juicer will work better for this recipe as it will not tear the membrane sections of the limes, allowing the lime juice to be a little sweeter and less bitter tasting. Rinsing the onion removes some of the oil from the onion slices, making the onion a little more mild, while still maintaining the crispness of the raw onions.

Cozumel Shrimp Cocktail

Served at Señor Frijoles Mexican Restaurant in Key Largo, this shrimp cocktail, served with fresh avocado in a margarita glass, makes a perfect light lunch or impressive appetizer to kick off a great meal.

Makes 2 servings

Ingredients:

14 large shrimp, peeled, deveined
4 cups water
3 tablespoons Sundowners' Black Caesar's Blackening Spice (recipe page 73)
1 bowl of ice with water (an ice bath for the shrimp)
½ medium red tomato, ripe, but firm, diced
¼ yellow onion, diced
1 tablespoon cilantro, chopped
½ teaspoon salt
4 tablespoons ketchup
1 avocado, cut into ¼ inch cubes
3 Key limes, juiced (or 1 Persian lime)
2 tostada shells

Preparation:

Place water and Old Bay in a pot, and bring to a boil. Add shrimp and boil for approximately 3 minutes (until shrimp are white throughout). Remove shrimp from water immediately and place in ice bath to stop the cooking process. Place all ingredients except the shrimp into a mixing bowl. Chop 4 shrimp. Place tomato mixture into margarita glasses and sprinkle chopped shrimp on top of mixture. Hang 5 shrimp off the side of each margarita glass, and serve with tostada shells on the side.

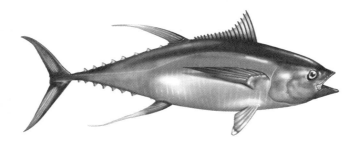

Tuna Poke

Originally from Hawaii, the word "poke" translates into little pieces of fish. After a fisherman would sell his fillets, he would make his dinner of poke from the scraps. Poke has been showing up in menus all over the Keys, and sushi grade tuna is the favorite of them all. Great as an appetizer or a light summer meal.

Makes 2 servings

Ingredients:

    1 pound raw, sushi grade tuna, cut into ¾ inch cubes
    2 tablespoons of sesame oil
    1 tablespoon of black and white sesame seeds
    2 tablespoons of Sriracha hot sauce (more if you like it spicier)
    2 tablespoons soy sauce
    2 tablespoons scallions, chopped
    2 Key limes, juiced and zested
    1 Haas avocado, diced
    1 small white onion, chopped

Preparation:

Place all ingredients into a mixing bowl and mix well. Serve this dish as soon as it is prepared, to taste the freshness of each of the ingredients.

Shrimp Remoulade

The secret to great shrimp is cooking the shrimp until they are *just* done. Shrimp overcook very easily, so it is important that shrimp be removed from heat just before they are medium well, so they can continue cooking while "resting." This dish is a special at Ballyhoo's Historic Seafood Grille in Rock Harbor. The shrimp are cooked and then allowed to marinate in the sauce. The result: tangy, crisp shrimp with a twist.

Makes 2 servings

Ingredients:

14 large shrimp, peeled, deveined
Remoulade Sauce (see below)
Sundowners' Black Caesar's Blackening Spice

Preparation:

Place water and Sundowners' Black Caesar's Blackening Spice in a pot, and bring to a boil. Add shrimp and boil for approximately 3 minutes (until shrimp are white throughout). Remove shrimp from water immediately and place in ice bath to stop the cooking process. Remove cooled shrimp from ice bath and place shrimp into Remoulade sauce. Refrigerate for at least 2 hours and serve.

Remoulade Sauce

Ingredients:

4 cups water
3 tablespoons Sundowners' Black Caesar's Blackening Spice (recipe page 73)
1 tablespoon Zatarain's Creole Mustard (or other spicy brown mustard)
½ teaspoon paprika
¼ teaspoon cayenne pepper
¼ teaspoon salt
¼ cup chopped green onions
1 dash Tabasco
2 tablespoons parsley, chopped
2 tablespoons cilantro, chopped
¼ cup mayonnaise
2 tablespoons vegetable oil
4 tablespoons ketchup
2 cloves garlic, minced

Place ingredients into a mixing bowl and mix well.

Rosemary & Garlic Grilled Shrimp

Another great shrimp recipe from Marker 88. Rosemary-skewered shrimp, marinated with Key lime, garlic, wine and olive oil.

Makes 4 servings

Ingredients:

16-20 large shrimp with the shell on
16-20 sprigs of rosemary (enough to skewer shrimp)
½ cup olive oil
¼ cup of dry white wine
6 cloves garlic, chopped
4 Key limes, sliced into wheels (or 1 Persian lime sliced)
salt & pepper to taste

Preparation:

Cut and soak rosemary sprigs in water, so that they will not burn as quickly when you place them on the barbecue grill. Place shrimp, oil, wine, garlic, Key lime wheels, and salt and pepper into a large Ziplock bag or into a bowl to marinate. Refrigerate for at least 2 hours, stirring occasionally. Remove shrimp from marinade and skewer. Pre-heat barbecue grill to medium high. Grill shrimp for approximately 3 minutes per side, until shrimp are almost white throughout. Remove from heat and allow shrimp to "rest" for 1-2 minutes before serving.

Shrimp Cargot
(Like Escargot, only with shrimp!)

The creaminess of the Havarti cheese goes really well with these shrimp. Make sure to serve this appetizer with plenty of crusty French bread on the side to soak up the extra sauce and cheese. For an added delight, substitute fresh Florida lobster meat for the shrimp.

Makes 2 servings

Ingredients:

- 12 large shrimp, peeled, deveined, and tails removed
- 4 ounces butter
- 2 ounces dry white wine
- 4 slices of Havarti cheese
- 1 teaspoon parsley, chopped

Preparation:

Preheat oven to 350° F. Place butter in a medium sauté pan over medium heat until butter is melted. Add wine, parsley and shrimp and sauté for 2-3 minutes per side, until shrimp are white on outside and medium-rare inside. Remove from heat. Move to an ovenproof dish large enough to hold shrimp and sauce. Cover shrimp with Havarti slices and place in oven until Havarti is melted. Remove from oven, let dish rest for 1-2 minutes, and serve.

Garlic & Beer Marinated Peel & Eat Shrimp

The next time you are having a party, try this variation of peel-and-eat shrimp. Suck the tails then peel and eat the shrimp! Garlicky, great, and a little messy, they are sure to be a hit with your guests.

Makes 8 - 10 servings

Ingredients:

- 2 pounds large Key West pink shrimp with the shell on
- 2 bottles dark beer
- 2 tablespoons chopped garlic in oil
- 2 tablespoons Sundowners' Black Caesar's Blackening Spice (recipe page 73)
- 8 cups water
- 3 tablespoons butter

Preparation:

Place shrimp, beer, garlic, and blackening spice into a large bowl. Mix until all shrimp are well coated with marinade. Place in refrigerator and marinate for at least an hour, tossing shrimp occasionally. Pour shrimp and marinade into a large sauce pot and add enough water to cover shrimp. Add butter and place pot on stove over medium high heat. Cook shrimp until shrimp are white throughout, and remove from heat. Strain and top with garlic butter sauce, recipe below. Serve and enjoy!

Garlic Butter Sauce

Amazing. Use this sauce on the shrimp above, or as the base for a great shrimp scampi.

Ingredients:

- ¼ pound butter
- 1 tablespoon Sundowners' Black Caesar's Blackening Spice (recipe page 73)
- 2 rounded tablespoons chopped garlic in oil
- ¼ cup dry white wine

Preparation:

Place butter into a small sauté pan and place on stove on medium-high heat. Once butter has melted, add white wine, blackening spice and chopped garlic. Once mixture begins to boil, reduce heat to medium and continue to sauté for 4-5 minutes until garlic has begun to turn brown, and to give the wine a chance to reduce.

Charbroiled Oysters

Ballyhoo's Historic Seafood Grille features these delicious oysters, fresh from the barbecue grill. They are best when you put them on a grill that is really hot, and the flames wrap around the side of the oyster.

Makes 24 -30 oysters

Ingredients:

- 24-30 fresh oysters, shucked, drained and cleaned
- ¼ cup freshly grated Parmesan cheese
- ¼ cup freshly grated Pecorino Romano cheese
- ½ cup parsley

Garlic Butter

- 1 cup butter, room temperature
- 2 tablespoons garlic, chopped fine
- ½ teaspoon fresh ground black pepper

Preparation:

Melt the butter with garlic and pepper in a large sauté pan. Mix Parmesan and Romano cheeses in a small bowl. Spoon some of the melted butter mixture onto each oyster. Add a pinch of cheese and a pinch of parsley to each oyster. Place oysters on grill (pre-heated to medium high). Grill oysters until they are hot and bubbly and the cheese has begun to "puff," approximately 6-8 minutes.

Wasabi-Mango Puree

Try this puree as a spicy "mirror" under grilled or blackened fish, or under crispy cornmeal-fried oysters.

Makes 2 servings (or enough for 20-30 oysters)

Ingredients:

- 1 medium ripe mango, cut into cubes
- 1 teaspoon prepared wasabi powder

Preparation:

Placed in blender or food processor and blend until smooth.

Pimento Cheese

Pimento cheese is served throughout the south, and is great on an adult grilled cheese, as a spread for crackers, or as a dip for veggies. Pimentos are typically pickled red cherry peppers, but for this recipe, I use fresh roasted red bell peppers. The roasted red peppers are sweeter than the cherry peppers and give the cheese a little more flavor.

Ingredients:

- 3 ounces cream cheese, room temperature
- 1 cup grated Monterey jack
- 1 cup grated cheddar cheese
- ½ cup mayonnaise
- ¼ teaspoon garlic powder
- ¼ teaspoon cayenne pepper
- ¼ teaspoon onion powder
- 1 red pepper, roasted and diced
- ½ jalapeño, roasted and diced
    (Optional. Use the same process as roasting red peppers below.)
- Salt and pepper to taste

Preparation:

Place all ingredients into a large bowl, and mix well. Typically a countertop mixer or a hand mixer work well for this recipe. Season with salt and pepper to taste. While you can use this immediately, I typically refrigerate it for an hour or so before serving.

Roasting Red Peppers:

Preheat oven to 400° F. Remove seeds from pepper and place peppers on a lightly greased cookie sheet. Bake for 10-15 minutes or until the skin of the pepper has turned black. Remove pepper from oven, and place in a stainless steel bowl. Cover with saran wrap and allow pepper to cool. Skin should be easy to remove from pepper. Cut pepper into strips and serve.

Mignonette Sauce for Raw Oysters

One of the greatest ways to enjoy raw oysters is with a mignonette sauce, made with fresh-chopped shallots or sweet onions and red wine vinegar. Try this sauce with lobster cocktail too!

Makes about ½ cup

Ingredients:

- ½ cup of red wine vinegar
- 2 tablespoons shallots finely chopped (or you can use sweet onions)
- 1 teaspoon parsley, chopped
- ½ tablespoon black pepper, coarsely ground
- Kosher salt to taste

Preparation:

Mix all ingredients in a small bowl, and refrigerate for at least 2 hours before serving.

Ponzu Sauce for Raw Oysters

Ponzu means "various citrus juices," and the flavor of this sauce with oysters is amazing. I really enjoy this sauce when paired up with a fresh raw oyster, like the thick shelled Kumamoto oyster.

Makes about ½ cup

Ingredients:

- 4 tablespoons soy sauce
- 2 tablespoons Key lime juice
- 1 tablespoon lemon juice
- 3 teaspoons rice vinegar
- Dashi powder (prepare enough to make 3 tablespoons of Dashi stock) optional.

Preparation:

Mix all ingredients in a small bowl, and refrigerate for at least 2 hours before serving.

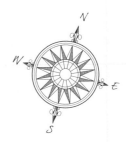

Feeding the Tarpon

One of the coolest things to do in the Keys is to feed the tarpon off of the docks of local restaurants. Tarpon, which can grow to almost 300 pounds, are considered one of the great saltwater game fishes, and are prized not only for their size, but also for their fight and spectacular jumping ability. To feed, tarpon typically hunt at night, and swallow their prey whole, since they have no real teeth, thus making them relatively safe to feed. You do have to be careful, however, because even without teeth, their "sandpaper" jaws can still leave a nasty mark, or scrape, on those who try to feed them by hand.

Here at Robbie's of Islamorada (above), the tarpon are as famous for relieving tourists of their watches, another by product of feeding them by hand, as they are for their aggressiveness. More than one Rolex has been lost by feeding tarpon by hand… so be careful!

Crab Cakes with Pommery Mustard Sauce

Great crab cakes are just plain hard to find. The secret to make a great crab cake is in the bread crumbs, you just need a tiny little bit, like the recipe from Sundowners Restaurant in Key Largo, below!

Makes 4 servings

Ingredients:

- 1 pound jumbo lump blue crab meat
- 1 egg
- 2 teaspoons Worcestershire sauce
- 1 tablespoon whole grain mustard
- ¼ teaspoon dry mustard
- 2 tablespoons mayonnaise
- 1 teaspoon lemon juice
- 1 tablespoon melted butter
- 1 teaspoon parsley, fresh chopped (or flakes)
- 1 teaspoon Sundowners' Black Caesar's Blackening Spice (recipe page 73)
- ½ cup plus 3 tablespoons panko bread crumbs
- oil for frying

Pommery Mustard Sauce

- ¼ cup whole grain mustard
- ½ cup heavy cream
- salt and pepper to taste

Preparation:

Mix all ingredients except crab meat and bread crumbs by hand, in a large bowl. Add crab meat and the ½ cup bread crumbs. Mix very gently, as you want to leave the jumbo lump crab meat as whole lumps. Form into 4-oz. crab cakes. Refrigerate the crab cakes for at least 1 hour to help them "set up."

Pour remaining bread crumbs onto a plate and press crab cakes onto the remaining bread crumbs on both the top and the bottom. Preheat oven to 350°. Pour some vegetable oil into a medium sized sauté pan, so that there is a ¼ inch of oil in the pan. Place the pan over medium heat, and heat until the oil reaches approximately 350°, or until the oil is "hot." Reduce heat to medium and place crab cakes in frying oil. Fry for one (1) minute on each side just to brown the bread crumbs.

Remove crab cakes from stove, drain off most of the oil, and place crab cakes in oven for 10 minutes (or until hot inside). While crab cakes are in the oven, place mustard sauce, heavy cream, and salt in pepper in sauté pan over medium-high heat and reduce until sauce is half its original volume (stirring constantly). Remove from heat and pour onto a plate or serving dish. Remove crab cakes from the oven and place on top of the mustard sauce. Enjoy!

How Sundowners Began

Sundowners Restaurant was built and opened in 1985 as an open-air restaurant on Florida Bay. My father, Bob Stoky Sr., loved to fish, and he wanted to open a restaurant where guests could enjoy fish the way he liked it — fresh and flavorful. Almost every day, my father would be close to the front door, welcoming guests, and being the host.

Over the years, glass doors were added to Sundowners to provide both inside and outside dining, and the menu has evolved, but the fish still comes in fresh almost every day, the preparations are still flavorful, and there are still Stoky family members on the property to make sure that everyone is happy.

Hot Blue Crab Dip

This crab dip is a party favorite at Marker 88, and is on almost every appetizer buffet that is booked at the restaurant. The secret, as always, is high quality, jumbo lump crab. Try this for your next party or get together.

Makes 4 cups

Ingredients:

- 1 pound jumbo lump blue crab meat
- 1 cup pepper jack cheese, grated
- 1 cup mayonnaise
- ½ cup grated Parmesan cheese
- 6 garlic cloves, roasted & chopped
- 3 tablespoons of Worcestershire sauce
- 2 tablespoons Key lime juice
- 1 teaspoon Sriracha sauce
- ½ teaspoon Coleman's dry mustard
- salt and pepper to taste

Preparation:

Preheat oven to 325° F. Mix cheese, mayonnaise, garlic, Worcestershire, Key lime juice, Sriracha sauce, Coleman's dry mustard, and salt and pepper in a mixing bowl. Fold crab into mixture, being careful not to over mix and break up the lumps of crab. Place mixture in an oven-proof baking dish. Cover with aluminum foil and bake for 40 minutes. Serve with toast points and roasted jalapeño pepper slices.

Key Lime Mustard Sauce for Stone Crabs

The entire stone crab industry was founded in Miami, Florida and today, this fishery is one of the largest fisheries in the State. Stone crabs are said to be sustainable, because only the claws are harvested from the crab, and the crab is thrown back into the sea to grow new claws. Most interesting about stone crabs is that they can only be harvested in warm water and must be cooked before being placed on ice. This is the only way to keep the meat from sticking to the shell. Traditionally, stone crabs are served cold. Try them with the mustard sauce recipe below.

Makes 4 servings

Ingredients:

    1 cup mayonnaise
    1 tablespoon Coleman's Dry Mustard (add more if you like it spicier)
    2 teaspoons Worcestershire sauce
    1 teaspoon A-1 Sauce
    4 teaspoons Key lime juice
    salt and pepper to taste

Preparation:

Mix all ingredients and chill for at least 1 hour before serving.

Tartar Sauce

Great with fried fish, this sauce is pretty much a staple of Keys home cooking. Try the simple Keys version, or spice it up a little with the optional fresh, chopped dill or the chopped capers.

Makes 4 servings

Ingredients:

    1 cup mayonnaise
    1 tablespoon sweet relish
    1 tablespoon dill relish
    1 tablespoon Key lime juice
    salt and pepper to taste
    (optional: 1 teaspoon fresh dill, chopped, or 1 teaspoon chopped capers)

Preparation:

Mix all ingredients and chill for at least 1 hour before serving.

Pickled Vegetable Salsa

I usually try to make everything fresh, but this salsa is so quick and easy to make when you use bottles of pickled vegetables versus making your own, that it is one of my exceptions to the rule.

Makes 4 servings

Ingredients:

- 2 jars of Jardiniere pickled vegetables, drain off half of the juice
- ½ onion, coarsely chopped
- 3 tomatoes, chopped into cubes
- 3 Key limes, juiced
- 2 jalapeños, coarsely chopped

Preparation:

Place all ingredients into a food processor, and pulse until chopped and well blended. Serve with chips or as a topping to fresh blackened fish.

Lobster Mango Guacamole

This guacamole is great when it is made with Haas avocados and fresh mangos. There are two ways to serve the lobster in this dish. You can mix it in with the guacamole, or you can pile the chopped lobster on top of the guacamole to really increase the wow factor. Either way, this dish is a real winner.

Makes 4 servings

Ingredients:

- 1 6-ounce lobster tail
- 2 Haas avocados, ripe
- 1 small mango, diced
- ½ yellow onion, diced
- 2 tablespoons fresh cilantro, chopped
- 1 fresh jalapeño, chopped
- 2 Key limes, juiced
- ½ teaspoon garlic powder
- ½ teaspoon salt

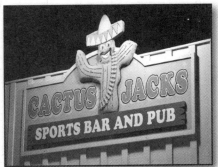

Preparation:

Place lobster tail in a pot of boiling water and cook for 3-4 minutes, until lobster meat is white throughout. Remove from water immediately and chill in a bowl full of ice and water to stop the cooking process. Mix avocados, mango, onion, cilantro, jalapeños, Key lime juice, garlic powder, and salt. Remove lobster meat from shell and chop coarsely. Mix with guacamole mixture or place on top of guacamole and serve with tortilla chips. Olé!

50 | **Recipes & Tall Tales from Legendary Restaurants of the Florida Keys**

Piña Colada Chicken Skewers

These skewers just remind me of the islands. The sugar in the cream of coconut and the tartness of the pineapple juice really add flavor to the chicken. My favorite way to prepare these is to use chicken tenders and to cut the tenders into 1-inch cubes, and then to stack the cubes on hickory-marinated skewers. The flavor is amazing.

Makes 6 servings

Ingredients:

- 2 pounds chicken tenders, cut into 1-inch cubes
- 8 ounces of Coco Lopez cream of coconut
- 15 ounces pineapple juice
- 18-20 4" bamboo skewers
- 1 cup hickory chips
- 1 fresh, pineapple, peeled, cored and cut into 1-inch cubes

Preparation:

Place the hickory chips and bamboo skewers into a pot of water, and boil skewers for at least 15 minutes. Remove from heat, and allow water to cool, before removing skewers. Salt and pepper chicken tender chunks, and place in a Ziplock bag with the cream of coconut and pineapple juice. Shake bag well, and refrigerate for at least an hour. Remove skewers from hickory water, and put 3 cubes of chicken on each skewer. Finish each skewer with a fresh pineapple chunk. Pre-heat barbecue grill and place chicken skewers on grill. Grill chicken for 3-4 minutes per side, or until chicken is cooked throughout. Remove from heat and serve.

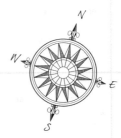

Chipotle Barbecue Sauce

A great barbecue sauce for twice cooked chipotle barbecued wings, or for use on barbecued shrimp. For barbecued shrimp I recommend using shrimp with the shells on and brushing the shells with the barbecue sauce. It makes for messy eating, but really yummy shrimp!

Makes approximately 2 cups

Ingredients:

- 2 tablespoons olive oil
- 1/2 medium yellow onion, chopped
- 2 heads of garlic, chopped
- 2 tablespoons Worcestershire
- 1 tablespoon chili powder
- 2 teaspoons cumin
- 1 cup ketchup
- ¾ cup dark brown sugar, firmly packed
- ¼ cup soy sauce
- 1 cup apple cider vinegar
- 2 tablespoons A-1 Sauce
- 2 tablespoons chipotle peppers, chopped with adobo sauce.

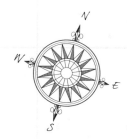

Preparation:

Heat the oil in a saucepan over medium heat. Add onions, garlic, Worcestershire, cumin, and chili powder to pan and sauté until onions begin to wilt. Add the malt vinegar, stirring and scraping the bottom of the saucepan to release all of the flavor of the spices. Add the rest of the ingredients, stir, and simmer until sauce thickens, approximately five minutes. Transfer barbecue sauce to a food processor and blend until smooth. Refrigerate for up to 3 days, and use just as you would any store-bought barbecue sauce.

Twice-Cooked Chipotle Barbecued Wings

Everyone has their favorite wing recipe, and this is mine. Cooking the wings twice seals in the juiciness and the flavor of the spices. There are a few steps to this recipe, but feel free to bake the wings a day or so in advance, and then just barbecue them on the day you're going to eat them. If you like wings, you are going to love these!

Makes 6 servings

Ingredients:

- 4-5 pounds of chicken wings (or drumettes)
- ½ cup olive oil
- ¼ cup paprika (I prefer smoked paprika, but regular will work too)
- 2 teaspoons salt
- 1 ½ teaspoons cayenne pepper
- 2 teaspoons white pepper
- 2 tablespoons coarse ground black pepper
- 2 tablespoons chili powder
- 2 tablespoons granulated garlic
- 2 tablespoons oregano
- 2 tablespoons cumin

Preparation:

Preheat oven to 350° F. Place oil and spices into a large bowl, and mix well. Toss wings in spice mix until wings are well coated with spices. Place wings on a large baking pan and bake for 30 minutes, or until wings reach an internal temperature of 165° F. Remove from oven and cool. Place in refrigerator for up to 3 days.

To cook the wings again (twice cooked):

Place wings on a hot barbecue grill and grill for about 3 minutes per wing (you only have to reheat the wings). Brush wings with Chipotle Barbecue Sauce, recipe on facing page, and close lid for approximately 1 minute, or until sauce begins to bubble on wings. Remove wings from grill, kick back, and enjoy.

Appetizers | 53

Pineapple Plantations - Plantation Key

The majority of the Upper Keys were uninhabited until Capt. Ben Baker, a Key West wrecker, single-handedly created the profitable pineapple boom period for the Upper Keys in the mid-to-late nineteeth century. Using pineapple "slips" imported from Cuba, Capt. Baker was harvesting over 50,000 pineapples a year from the Florida Keys in 1876, using slash-and-burn methods to clear vast areas for pineapple plantations. Even with the small amount of rain that we receive in the Florida Keys, the pineapple plantations thrived, eventually yielding approximately 7,000 pineapples an acre. Pineapple plantations sprouted up all over the Keys, but were especially prevalent just south of Tavernier Creek, in the area known today as Plantation Key.

In 1906, a devastating hurricane ravaged the Florida Keys, and that pretty much put an end to the pineapple plantations on Plantation Key.

This old wooden fence in shows a pineapple motif. Photo by Karen Beal.

Grilled Avocados

In the summertime, avocados are almost as plentiful in South Florida and in parts of the Keys as the mosquito. They are everywhere! So we have come up with all sorts of ways to have avocados. There is even a winery just north of the Keys that sells avocado wine. Anyway, this recipe is fast, easy, and delicious, so give it a try.

Makes 4-6 servings

Ingredients:

2-3 ripe Florida avocados
4 tablespoons extra virgin olive oil
1 teaspoon garlic powder
2 Key limes (cut in half to squeeze)
1 tablespoon Tabasco or other hot sauce
salt & pepper to taste

Preparation:

Preheat barbecue grill. Cut avocados into thick wedges, leaving skin on. Mix 2 tablespoons olive oil with hot sauce and brush each wedge with oil mixture. Sprinkle wedges with garlic powder, salt and pepper. Allow wedges to marinate for at least 15 minutes, then place on a hot barbecue grill. Grill wedges for 2-3 minutes per side. Remove from grill and remove skins. Drizzle slices with the remaining olive oil, and fresh-squeezed Key lime juice.

Baked Oysters Barrios

Everyone always says that you cannot eat oysters in months whose names do not contain "r," as in September through April, but this "rule of thumb" is simply not true. Great oysters are available almost any time of the year, and what better time to have oysters than during summer barbecues or get-togethers? Besides, oysters are party food. They're typically not the type of food that you make just for yourself. Anyway… this oyster dish was invented by Chef Salvador Barrios at Marker 88, and it is amazing. Give them a try for yourself!

Makes 24 oysters

Ingredients:

24 oysters, on the half shell
6 slices thick-cut, apple-smoked bacon, cut into 24 pieces
1 pound fresh mozzarella, cut into 24 cubes
3 Jalapeños cut into 24 slices (remove seeds if jalapeños are too hot)
1 bunch of cilantro
Salt and pepper to taste

Preparation:

Preheat oven to 375° F. Place shucked oysters onto a baking sheet. Top each oyster with a cube of mozzarella, a piece of bacon, and finish with a jalapeño slice. Add salt and pepper to taste. Place oysters into the oven and bake for approximately 10 minutes, or until bacon has begun to crisp and the mozzarella is "bubbly." Remove oysters from oven, garnish liberally with cilantro leaves and serve.

Marinated Tempura Shrimp with Florida Ponzu Dipping Sauce

Perfect for the summer, these shrimp are sure to be a hit with your friends and family. The citrus marinade adds a nice sweetness to the shrimp. The recipe is gluten free too, as we use rice flour for the shrimp. Try them out and let me know what you think.

Makes 2-3 Servings

Ingredients:

- 3-4 wooden skewers
- 12 large shrimp, peeled, deveined, with the tails removed
- 6-8 fresh broccoli florets
- 2-3 Florida oranges, juiced
- 3-4 Key limes, juiced
- 1 egg
- 1 cup rice flour (or all-purpose flour)
- 1 cup ice water
- 1 teaspoon sesame seeds
- Salt and pepper to taste
- Vegetable oil for frying
- Flour for dusting

Preparation:

Marinate the shrimp in orange and Key lime juice, for approximately 30 minutes before serving. Place 3-4 shrimp on each skewer, leaving a small amount of room between shrimp for even cooking. Mix water, flour, and egg in a shallow pan large enough to dip shrimp into. Heat vegetable oil in a frying pan, or small counter fryer, until oil reaches 375° F. Lightly dust shrimp with flour and then place shrimp into tempura batter. Gently place shrimp into hot oil and cook for 4-5 minutes, or until shrimp are white throughout. Do not overcook shrimp. Dip broccoli florets into tempura batter and fry for 3-4 minutes. Serve with Florida ponzu dipping sauce on the side.

Florida Ponzu Sauce

Ingredients:

- 2-3 Florida oranges, juiced
- 1-2 Key limes, juiced
- 1 teaspoon Sriracha hot sauce
- 3-4 green onions, sliced diagonally
- ¼ cup soy sauce
- ¼ cup rice wine vinegar
- 1 teaspoon sugar

Preparation:

Place all ingredients into a small bowl and mix well. Add additional Sriracha if you like your ponzu spicy. Enjoy!

Preserved Key Lime Vinaigrette

Try this tasty Key lime vinaigrette on a hearts of palm salad or drizzle it over grilled shrimp or squid. The amount of oil and vinegar will vary with the size of your Key limes and flavor preferences.

Ingredients:

4 whole preserved Key limes,
   or other preserved citrus fruit
1 large shallot, diced
2 teaspoon Dijon mustard
½ cup champagne vinegar
1 ½ cups extra virgin olive oil)
sea salt or Kosher salt to taste

Preparation:

Remove seeds from Key limes and place into a food processor or blender. Blend until smooth. Add diced shallot, mustard, vinegar, and extra virgin olive oil and process until well blended. Add salt to taste.

Preserved Key Limes

Preserved limes have been used throughout history since they are easy to preserve, last a long time, and have a great flavor. Use them sparingly, as a little goes a long way. Chefs will often separate the flesh of the lime from the skin and will use the flesh and juice from the limes in sauces, while using the diced flesh as a garnish.

Ingredients:

6-8 Key limes
additional fresh lime juice
Kosher salt
12-16 ounce Mason jar, sanitized

Preparation:

Rinse Key limes with plenty of fresh water, then cut limes in half. Remove any visible seeds, and place limes into a Mason jar, skin side up. Place a teaspoon of salt in the jar on top of each whole lime. Place the next Key lime into the jar, alternating the limes so they will stack neatly into the Mason jar. Continue stacking until no more limes will fit in the jar. It is okay to press the limes so that you can stack more into the jar. Once the jar is filled and salted, fill the remaining space inside the jar with additional fresh Key lime juice, so that all of the limes are covered with juice. Place lid on jar, and tighten. Place jar in a cool, low-light area, and shake every few days to help to incorporate the salt into the lime juice. Typically, the limes are ready in 12-14 days, once the skins have become soft, however they can be stored for up to 3-4 months as long as you have done a good job cleaning and salting them.

Paradise... Legal or Illegal?

Key Largo. Famous for sunsets, conch shells, sailfishing, and Key lime pie has been paradise to many people for many things over the years. In the 17th century, Black Caesar found paradise and called Key Largo home to himself and his pirating crew, burying over $17 million in treasure somewhere around Key Largo. In the early 1900s, Key Largo was a paradise to rum runners who sought refuge in Key Largo's sounds, while waiting for nightfall to continue their rum running route north to Miami or south to Key West. In the mid-to-late 1970s, drug runners found Key Largo to be a paradise of off-loading spots for drugs headed from the Caribbean basin to Miami and the rest of the United States.

The Florida Keys, with over 200 miles of mostly unprotected coastline, sparse population, and two roads that lead into Miami, was the perfect spot for drug runners who would come ashore under the cover of darkness, quickly unload their merchandise into waiting vehicles, and then run straight out of the Florida Keys, headed for mainland USA.

Sleek and fast, "cigarette" type racing boats, were the boats of choice for drug runners, whose boats at the time were substantially faster than that of law enforcement. These boats, with their shallow drafts, were able to ply both the offshore waters of Key Largo, as well as the backcountry waters of Florida Bay. Drug running quickly became the largest industry in the Florida Keys, and locals, who had extensive knowledge of the waters of the Florida Keys, became invaluable to drug runners interested in protecting their investment in marijuana bales known as "square grouper." The locals' use of narrow, winding mangrove channels, shallow "cuts" across mud banks, and hidden marinas continued to fuel the growth of the drug trade.

Blackwater Sound, just behind Señor Frijoles Restaurant was the site of many drug chases during this time, and yielded some of the largest drug busts in South Florida. Word from the "Coconut Telegraph," the local rumor mill, was that the marina next door, Deep 6 Marina, with easy U.S.1 access and aboat basin concealed from both U.S.1 and the bay, was the place of many drug runs. One local was making so much money during this time that he found it necessary to purchase two jets with cash, leading to his arrest and incarceration. The Coconut Telegraph told of money replacing insulation in the walls of many Keys homes.

Black Caesar's fortune has never been found, and many homes have been remodeled in search of hidden cash, but today, paradise has returned to mostly sunsets, conch shells, sailfishing, Key Lime pie, and the occasional rum runner (a drink) or square grouper sandwich (a fish sandwich). And here you are, discovering your own paradise in Key Largo... may it be a legal one!

SOUPS AND SALADS & SALAD DRESSINGS

Tastes of the Islands!

All about Conchs!

The moniker "conch" (prounounced konk) is used to describe residents of the Florida Keys who were born here, with those who have lived in the Florida Keys for more than seven years being referred to as "fresh water conchs." It is a badge of honor for many Keys residents. Originally, however, the term "conch" was a derogatory term applied to native Bahamians by American Revolutionists loyal to the crown, due to their diet of mollusk found throughout the shallow Bahamian waters. As Bahamians began to inhabit the Keys in the 1900s, they brought the term "conch" with them, and today, the term is applied generally to all residents of the Florida Keys.

Honorary Conchs

Today, the Mayor of Monroe County is authorized by the Monroe County Commission to grant Honorary Conch certificates to those whose mission helps to serve the Keys. These awards have been given to heads of state, politicians, actors, activists, and just generally good people throughout the world.

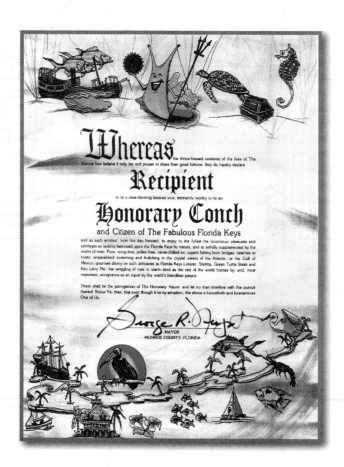

Traditional Conch Chowder

Traditionally, conch chowder is red, or tomato based. This is the chowder that is served throughout the Caribbean, and is typically the type that you will find on most menus throughout the Keys. A rich, red chowder, chock full of conch, potatoes and spices, is nicely complimented, with pale dry sherry on the side. Some people drink the sherry, I prefer to add it to my chowder.

Makes 8 - 10 servings

Ingredients:

- ½ pound bacon, cut into cubes
- 2 onions, diced
- 2 pounds conch, ground
- 1 green pepper, diced
- 2 stalks of celery, chopped
- 6 large potatoes, diced
- 1 6-ounce can tomato paste
- 1 15-ounce can diced tomatoes
- 4 bay leaves
- 1 tablespoon oregano
- 3 tablespoons thyme
- 1 tablespoon all spice (optional)
- 3 carrots, diced
- 1 teaspoon cayenne pepper (add more if you like it spicy)
- salt & pepper to taste

Preparation:

Place bacon and onions in a 4-quart pot, and sauté until onions are soft. Add ground conch, green peppers, celery and continue to sauté for 4-5 minutes, stirring to prevent burning. Add the rest of the ingredients, stir, and reduce heat to simmer. Add water, or clam juice, throughout the cooking process, as necessary, to keep the chowder thick, but not too thick. Simmer for 1-2 hours, stirring occasionally, until potatoes are soft. Serve with spiced pale dry sherry and hot sauce on the side.

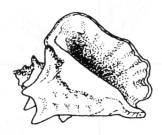

64 | **Recipes & Tall Tales from Legendary Restaurants of the Florida Keys**

White Conch Chowder

Not traditional, but very good, this chowder is prepared basically the same way that clam chowder is prepared, except that you substitute conch for the clams. The chopped leeks in this chowder add a nice flavor and texture to the soup.

Makes 4 servings

Ingredients:

¼ lb. smoked bacon, chopped
1 onion, finely diced
4 cloves garlic, minced
½ leek, finely chopped
1 carrot, finely diced
2 cups clam juice (may substitute fish stock)
2 cups water
1 cup heavy cream
½ cup dry white wine
2 potatoes, diced
1 pound conch, ground
½ teaspoon cornstarch, dissolved in a little water
3 bay leaves
½ teaspoon ground cumin
2-3 dashes of Tabasco
salt, pepper and nutmeg to taste

Preparation:

Place bacon, onions, and garlic in a 4-quart pot and sauté over medium heat until the onions are soft. Add the leeks and carrots, and sauté for 2-3 minutes until leeks are soft. Add the remaining ingredients, reduce heat to simmer, and cook for 1-2 hours until the potatoes are soft.

Clam Chowder

A Sundowners' favorite, this chowder is chock full of clams. At Sundowners, we serve this soup in a sourdough bread bowl, with Seasoned Oyster Crackers (see page 68) and hot sauce on the side. Simply amazing.

Makes 5 servings

Ingredients:

- 3 teaspoons unsalted butter
- 6 slices apple-smoked bacon, chopped
- ½ cup yellow onion, diced
- ½ cup celery, diced
- ¼ teaspoon fresh thyme, finely chopped
- ¼ teaspoon fresh oregano, finely chopped
- 1 ½ cups clam broth
- ¼ teaspoon ground white pepper
- 2 potatoes, diced small
- 5 dashes of Tabasco (more if you like it spicy)
- 1 teaspoon Worcestershire
- 2 ½ cups clams, chopped
- 3 cups heavy cream
- 2 tablespoons cornstarch, dissolved in a little water

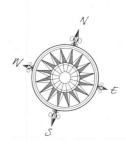

Preparation:

In a 4-quart pot, melt butter and sauté bacon until golden brown. Add diced onions and celery, and sauté until tender and translucent. Add clam broth, white pepper, Worcestershire sauce, Tabasco sauce, potatoes, and fresh herbs to pot. Cook for approximately 15 minutes to soften potatoes and incorporate flavors. Add heavy cream and chopped clams. Bring to a boil and thicken with cornstarch. Reduce heat immediately so as to not overcook the clams — it makes them tough.

Blue Crab Soup

Charleston, South Carolina is known for their She Crab Soup, made with flaked blue crabs and female blue crab roe, hence the name. Halfway between a bisque and a chowder, this flavorful soup is great when served with homemade garlic bread. While most of the lump blue crab meat on the market today comes from the Pacific, you can still get fresh blue crabs along Card Sound in north Key Largo, or from the fisherman over in Everglades City.

Makes 4 servings

Ingredients:

- 2 tablespoons unsalted butter
- 2 tablespoons all-purpose flour
- 2 cups milk
- ¾ cup pale dry sherry
- 1 ½ cups Half & Half cream
- 4 teaspoons onion, finely chopped or grated
- 4 teaspoons garlic, finely chopped
- ¼ teaspoon Key lime zest (or lemon zest)
- ½ pound of blue crab meat, flaked
- salt & white pepper to taste
- extra cayenne pepper to shake on top of soup

Preparation:

In a 4-quart, heavy stock pot, melt butter over low heat. Add flour and whisk until smooth -creating a white roux. Slowly add milk and Half & Half cream, stirring constantly. Cook for 3-4 minutes, until thickened. Add sherry, onions, garlic, salt, white pepper, and lemon zest. Bring mixture just to a boil and reduce heat to low. Add crab meat and simmer for 5 minutes. Do not allow the soup to boil. Remove from heat, place in serving bowls, top with cayenne pepper and serve with pale dry, or spiced, sherry on the side.

Hurricane Dipping Oil

This is the oil we serve at Marker 88 to dip the bread and focaccia into. Served warm with a touch of balsamic vinegar, this oil is much tastier than just the olive oil and vinegar served at most restaurants.

Makes 1 cup

Ingredients:

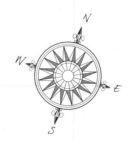

¾ cup of olive oil
1 tablespoon red pepper flakes
1 tablespoon fresh parsley, chopped
2 teaspoons fresh oregano, chopped
2 teaspoons fresh basil, chopped
1 teaspoon fresh rosemary, chopped
2 teaspoons garlic, chopped
¼ cup of balsamic vinegar
Kosher salt, to taste

Preparation:

Place oil and garlic in a sauté pan and sauté over medium-high heat until garlic begins to brown, reduce heat and all red pepper flakes, parsley, oregano, basil, rosemary, and Kosher salt. Simmer for approximately 4 minutes, remove from heat, add balsamic vinegar, stir, and serve.

Seasoned Oyster Crackers

These no-cook croutons, famous in the south, make a great snack, or a delicious addition to soups or salads. When stored in an airtight container crackers will last for 2-3 days.

Makes a bowl full of oyster crackers!

Ingredients:

2 bags of oyster crackers (or 4 bags of saltines)
2 packages dry buttermilk ranch dressing
¾ cup of canola oil
1 teaspoon fresh dill weed, chopped
1 tablespoon of crushed red pepper

Preparation:

Place buttermilk ranch dressing, oil, lemon pepper, dill weed, garlic salt, and crushed red pepper into a bowl and mix well. Place crackers into a large container or Ziplock bag and pour dressing mix over crackers. Store crackers in an airtight container. If crackers get stale, bake in oven for 2-3 minutes on a cookie sheet.

Garlic Croutons

While searching for the greatest croutons, I have tried many different recipes. Some fancy, some with tons of ingredients, but the best croutons that I could come up with had just a few ingredients, and a trick -softened butter. Try them for yourself if you don't believe me.

Makes a bunch of croutons!

Ingredients:

½ loaf of Cuban or Italian bread, cut into cubes, and left out to get stale
¼ pound of butter, left out at room temperature until soft
4 tablespoons garlic, chopped
1 teaspoon fresh oregano, chopped
½ teaspoon paprika
½ teaspoon onion powder
½ teaspoon garlic powder
½ teaspoon salt

Preparation:

Preheat oven to 250° F. Place bread cubes on a cookie sheet so that none overlap and place in oven for 30 minutes. Place butter, garlic and seasonings in a bowl and mix. It is very important that the butter is room temperature, and the consistency of mayonnaise. The trick is, if the butter is too hard or too soft, this recipe will not work. Remove the croutons from the oven, and allow them to cool to room temperature. Mix croutons in butter mixture, and place back on cookie sheet. Place back in oven for 10-15 minutes until most of the butter is cooked into the croutons. Remove croutons from oven and allow them to cool to room temperature.

Spiced Pale Dry Sherry

At Sundowners, we like to surprise our guests with the extra touch, so we created this spicy sherry for our guests. A little extra flavor and zing for our famous chowder.

Makes 1 jar

Ingredients:

11 ounces pale dry sherry
1 Scotch Bonnet pepper
1 small Mason jar with lid

Preparation:

Wash and clean mason jar well. Wash and clean the Scotch Bonnet pepper. Add sherry and scotch bonnet pepper to Mason jar. Cover tightly and store in a cool, dark place for 4-5 days, or until sherry is "spicy." Remove the pepper when the sherry is to your liking.

Soups, Salads & Salad Dressings | 69

Why is Ballyhoo's Legendary?

In the 1930s, the Florida Keys became known as a mecca for sportsfishermen from all over the world. Small fishing camps sprang up in the Keys to accommodate these groups of fishermen, who wanted comfortable sleeping quarters, great food, strong drink, camaraderie, and of course, outstanding fishing.

The fishermen, guided in their endeavors by locals, breakfasted, fished the morning, then came back into shore for a hearty lunch and a rest before resuming fishing in the afternoon. In the evening, they enjoyed another hearty meal followed by beer, cigars and tall tales from the day's adventures.

The Conch structure that today houses Ballyhoo's was one of the buildings from an early fishing camp. While many buildings have not survived the ravages of time and storms, Ballyhoo's Dade County pine structure has been lovingly preserved and restored so that you may enjoy the beamed ceilings and quaint atmosphere while feasting on the best seafood, steaks and sandwiches the Florida Keys has to offer. Ballyhoo's menu has evolved from traditional Conch favorites to current ones, and if you pay attention, you'll overhear some great fishing tales while you're there!

Ballyhoo's Jalapeño Cornbread

Sweet and a little spicy, these cornbread muffins are an excellent addition to any Keys-style meal. Light and flaky on the inside and a little crispy on the outside!

Makes 12 muffins (or one 9" cast iron skillet)

Ingredients:

- ¾ cup of cornmeal
- ¼ cup of all-purpose flour
- 1 teaspoon baking powder
- ½ teaspoon Kosher salt
- 2 tablespoons mangrove honey
- ¾ cup of low fat milk
- 1 large egg, beaten
- 2 ounces butter, melted and cooled
- 1 ½ cups, sweet corn kernels (fresh is best, frozen is okay too)
- 3 jalapeño peppers, seeded and diced

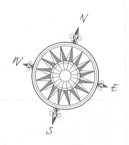

Preparation:

Preheat oven to 400° F. In a large bowl, mix together the cornmeal, flour, baking powder and salt. In another bowl mix the honey, milk, egg, and butter. Pour the wet ingredients into the dry ingredients and stir until all ingredients are just "wet," do not over stir. Fold in the sweet corn kernels and jalapeños. Butter a 9" cast iron skillet, or 12 medium-sized muffin pans, and pour the batter into the pans. Bake for approximately 30 minutes, or until a toothpick inserted into the center of the bread comes out clean.

Soups, Salads & Salad Dressings

Luau Bread

More "cake like" than the Luau Bread that we serve at Sundowners, this bread is great with dinner, or for breakfast, with homemade Mangrove honey butter.

Makes 1 Loaf

Ingredients:

    2 cups all-purpose flour
    1 teaspoon salt
    ½ teaspoon baking soda
    1 egg
    1 cup sugar
    ¼ cup sour cream
    1 8-ounce can crushed pineapple, drained & reserved
    1 tablespoon of the reserved pineapple juice

Preparation:

Combine dry ingredients with sour cream, pineapple and then add the pineapple juice. Spray the bottom of a loaf pan with cooking spray and turn the batter into the pan. Bake in 350° F preheated oven, for approximately 45 minutes. Test with a wooden skewer or toothpick... it should come out clean.

Mango Bread

Mangos are one of the Keys favorite fruits and we make practically everything with them. If you like mangos, then this sweet bread will definitely tackle your craving.

Makes 1 Loaf

Ingredients:

    2 cups flour
    2 teaspoons baking soda
    1 teaspoon salt
    1 cup sugar
    1 teaspoon cinnamon
    ½ cup raisins
    ¾ cup vegetable oil
    3 eggs
    2 chopped ripe mangos
    1 teaspoon vanilla extract

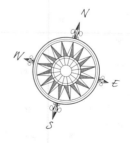

Procedure:

Combine all dry ingredients, then mix in oil, eggs, and vanilla extract. Mix well. Fold in mango chunks and pour into greased bread pan. Bake in a 325° oven for one hour. Test with a wooden skewer or toothpick...It should come out clean. Cool for 20 minutes.

Crispy Onion Straws for Salads, Burgers and more

These are the onion straws we serve on many of the salads at Sundowners. They are sweet, a little spicy and add an excellent texture to the dish. You can prepare these onion straws in advance and use them as you need them, as they will last for up to 3 days at room temperature.

Makes onion straws for at least 10 salads

Ingredients:

- 2 large yellow onions, sliced thin
- 2 cups all-purpose flour
- 4 tablespoons of Sundowners' Black Caesar's Blackening Spice (see recipe below)
- 4 quarts of oil for frying

Preparation:

Preheat oil to 350° F. In a large mixing bowl, mix flour and blackening spice. Toss onions in flour mixture and tap onions to remove any extra flour. Place in fryer and fry for approximately 2 minutes. Remove onion straws from fryer and dry on paper towels. Replace paper towels and store room temperature onion straws in an airtight container. Use on salads, burgers, chicken sandwiches, or on top of sesame-seared tuna.

Sundowners' Black Caesar's Blackening Spice

We use this on almost everything! A little on French fries or grilled shrimp, a lot for blackening fish and crabs, and a rub for steaks and roasts.

Ingredients:

- 1 teaspoon granulated garlic
- 2 teaspoon onion powder
- 2 teaspoon cayenne pepper
- ½ teaspoon ground mustard
- ½ teaspoon ground white pepper
- ½ teaspoon ground black pepper
- 2 teaspoon dried thyme
- 1 teaspoon dried oregano
- 1 teaspoon dried basil
- 2 tablespoon paprika
- 1 tablespoon Kosher salt

Preparation:

Combine all ingredients, store in an airtight container, and mix well before using.

You can also buy this spice mix at Sundowners in Key Largo, or on our website: www.SundownersRestaurant.com

The Mangroves of Key Largo

Mangroves are trees and shrubs that grow in salt water coastal habitats in the tropics and subtropics – mainly between latitudes 25° N and 25° S. The saltwater habitat created by mangroves is known as a mangal and includes the Red, Black, and White Mangrove trees. As you look out from Sundowners, it may appear there is land surrounding Blackwater Sound, when in actuality it is mud flats and shoals covered by mangroves without any dry land. A favorite activity in Key Largo is sea kayaking through the leafy canopied channels that form in the mangals.

The red mangrove is the most predominate in the Florida Keys and can grow to 25 or 30 feet tall. It is distinguished by the red-barked, finger-like prop roots that extend into the water. Through the years, man has used mangroves for many purposes. Fruits from the red mangrove are edible, and the leaves have been used to make tea, as a medicine, and as feed for livestock. Wood from the red mangrove is strong and water resistant. It's been used to make boats, furniture, pilings, and houses. The black mangrove's flower produces nectar and beekeepers place their hives nearby to produce the great-tasting, local honey Sundowners uses in its recipes. The bark was used for tannin and dyes, and charcoal was made from the dense wood of the black mangrove as well.

An estimated 75% of the game fish and 90% of the commercial fish species in south Florida depend on the mangrove system as well as many birds, reptiles, crustaceans, corals and seagrasses. The only enemy to these trees other than hurricanes and tropical storms, is man. Despite restoration efforts, developers and others have removed over half of the world's mangroves in recent times, therefore the Mangrove Protection Act made it illegal to destroy or damage them in the State of Florida in 1985.

Mangrove Honey-Lime Vinaigrette Dressing

Mangrove honey is local bee honey, made from the nectar of the mangrove blossom. The honey is sweet and earthy, and goes well with this dressing. If you think that all honeys are the same, think again. It's worth trying a few different types of honey before picking your favorite.

Ingredients:

- 1/3 cup vegetable oil
- 1/4 cup rice vinegar
- 1/4 cup mangrove honey (or other local honey)
- 2 1/2 teaspoons fresh Key lime juice
- 1 teaspoon sesame oil
- 1 1/2 teaspoons minced red bell peppers
- 1 1/2 teaspoon minced onion
- 1/4 teaspoon fresh ground black pepper
- 1 tablespoon chopped fresh cilantro
- 2 tablespoons Dijon Mustard
- salt and pepper to taste

Preparation:

Combine all ingredients in a microwave-proof bowl. Mix well. Place dressing in microwave and cook on high for approximately 1 minute, or until dressing begins to bubble. Remove from microwave and whisk until dressing begins to thicken, approximately 1 to 2 minutes. Cover and chill before serving.

Orange Dill Ranch Dressing

While I prefer to make ranch dressing from scratch, I cannot see getting all of the ingredients to make this dressing at home, when decent ranch dressings already exist at the store, so breaking my rule on making everything from scratch again, here's a quick-and-easy, great-tasting dressing that's ready in a flash.

Makes about 1 cup

Ingredients:

- 3/4 cup prepared buttermilk-ranch dressing
- 2 teaspoons grated orange rind
- 3 tablespoons fresh squeezed orange juice
- 2 teaspoons fresh dill, chopped

Preparation:

Place all ingredients in a bowl, and whisk. Chill for at least 1 hour before serving.

Mango Citrus Vinaigrette Dressing

One of the most copied and popular salads in the Keys is the Tropical Salad at Marker 88. Fresh baby greens topped with fresh tropical fruits and Marker 88's Mango Vinaigrette.

Makes enough for 4 salads

Ingredients:

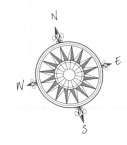

- ½ cup mango puree
- ½ tablespoon fresh orange juice
- 1 ½ tablespoons pineapple juice
- ½ tablespoon raspberry champagne vinegar
- 1 ½ tablespoons vegetable oil
- white pepper to taste

Preparation:

Place mango puree, orange juice, pineapple juice, and vinegar into a blender or food processor, and blend well. While blending, slowly add the oil to the dressing. Add white pepper to taste.

Toss with fresh greens and top with fresh tropical fruits and toasted coconut.

Oriental Dressing

This is the dressing that we use on the Oriental Tuna Salad at Sundowners. It is a great dressing for a salad with sesame-seared tuna or fresh, grilled fish.

Makes approximately 3 cups

Ingredients:

- ½ cup balsamic vinegar
- ½ cup soy sauce
- ¾ cup sugar
- 1 cup olive oil
- 4 tablespoons rice wine vinegar
- 1 ½ teaspoons ground ginger

Preparation:

Mix well. Cover, and chill before serving.

Thai Peanut Sauce

Ingredients:

¼ cup all-natural, no-sugar-added peanut butter
2 teaspoons soy sauce
1 tablespoon brown sugar
1 tablespoon Key lime juice
¼ cup coconut milk
¼ cup water
red chili flakes to taste
1 clove crushed garlic

Mix and serve warm; store refrigerated.

Pineapple Cole Slaw

Great for those warm summer days out on your boat at the sandbar off Islamorada, or at a barbecue on the beach, this coleslaw is a refreshing surprise from the ordinary.

Makes 6 - 8 servings

Ingredients:

½ small can crushed pineapple, keep half of the juice.
¾ cup of sour cream
½ teaspoon white wine vinegar
1 teaspoon Key lime juice
1 teaspoon Demura sugar
¼ teaspoon yellow mustard
Salt & pepper to taste
3 cups shredded cabbage
½ cup shredded carrots

Preparation:

In a large bowl, mix pineapple, pineapple juice, white vinegar, Key lime juice, Demura sugar, yellow mustard, salt, and pepper. Fold in sour cream, cover, and chill. When ready to serve, toss cabbage and carrots with dressing and serve.

Pretzel Bread

This wonderful bread, served warm, is a delight for young and old!

Makes 16 servings

Ingredients:

1 ½ cups warm water (approximately 115° F)
1 ¼ tablespoons sugar
2 teaspoons sea salt
¾ ounce package active dry yeast
22 ounces all-purpose flour, approximately 4 ½ cups
2 ounces unsalted butter, melted
vegetable oil
10 cups water
2/3 cup baking soda
1 large egg yolk beaten with 1 tablespoon water
pretzel salt

Preparation:

Combine the water, sugar and sea salt in the bowl of a dough mixer and sprinkle the yeast on top. Allow to sit for 5 minutes or until the mixture begins to foam. Add the flour and butter and, using the dough hook attachment, mix on low speed until well combined. Change to medium speed and knead until the dough is smooth and pulls away from the side of the bowl, approximately 4 to 5 minutes. Remove the dough from the bowl, clean the bowl and then oil it well with vegetable oil. Return the dough to the bowl, cover with plastic wrap and sit in a warm place for approximately 60 minutes or until the dough has doubled in size.

Preheat the oven to 450° F. Line 2 cookie sheets with parchment paper and lightly brush with the vegetable oil. Set aside. Add 10 cups of water to a large stock pot with the baking soda and bring to a boil. While water is boiling, turn the dough out onto a slightly oiled work surface and divide into 16 equal pieces, approximately 2 ounces in size. Roll each out until it is the shape of a small hot dog roll, and set aside.

Place the pretzel rolls into the boiling water one at a time, and boil for approximately 30 seconds. Remove them from the water using a large slotted spoon. Return to the half sheet pan, brush the top of each roll with the egg yolk mixture and sprinkle with pretzel salt. The more egg yolk you use, the browner the bread will be. Bake for approximately 12 to 14 minutes, or until rolls are dark brown in color. Remove from oven, allow to cool, and serve.

Crab Avocado Stack

A great salad, at Marker 88 we make this in a round three-inch salad form, by lining the form with plastic wrap, and then stacking the crab and avocado inside. Don't think that you have to do it like we do at Marker 88, this salad is still great just nicely piled on a plate or in a salad bowl.

Makes 4 salads

Ingredients:

  1 pound jumbo lump blue crab meat
  ¾ cup Remoulade dressing (see below)
  2 ½ cups mango, ripe peeled and diced into ½ inch pieces
  1 cup red bell pepper, diced
  1 tablespoon jalapeño pepper, seeded and chopped
  ¼ cup red onion, diced
  2 large ripe avocados, diced
  fresh basil as garnish

Preparation:

Mix the crab and Remoulade dressing, and chill. In a separate bowl, mix mangos, bell pepper, jalapeño, onions, and avocados. Spoon avocado mixture onto center of four small salad plates or bowls. Top each salad with the cold crab and Remoulade mixture. Garnish with fresh basil, and serve.

Remoulade Dressing

Ingredients:

  1 ¼ cup mayonnaise
  1 cup Creole mustard
  1 tablespoon chopped garlic
  1 scant teaspoon fresh lemon juice
  ½ teaspoon Worcestershire sauce
  ¼ teaspoon Tabasco sauce

Preparation:

Mix all ingredients well, cover and chill for at least 1 hour before serving.

Shoyu Salad Dressing

Another great Asian-inspired dressing. Perfect for a grilled fish salad, with fresh ingredients like cilantro, mint, orange segments, strawberries and avocado!

Ingredients:

- 1 small clove of garlic, halved and smashed
- ½ cup rice vinegar
- 2 tablespoons chopped onion
- 4 tablespoons soy sauce
- pinch of salt
- 2 tablespoons sugar
- ½ cup vegetable oil
- 4 teaspoons sesame oil
- 1 tablespoon pimento
- 10 black olives

Preparation:

Combine all ingredients into a blender and pulse until well blended. Refrigerate for at least one hour before serving.

Soups, Salads & Salad Dressings

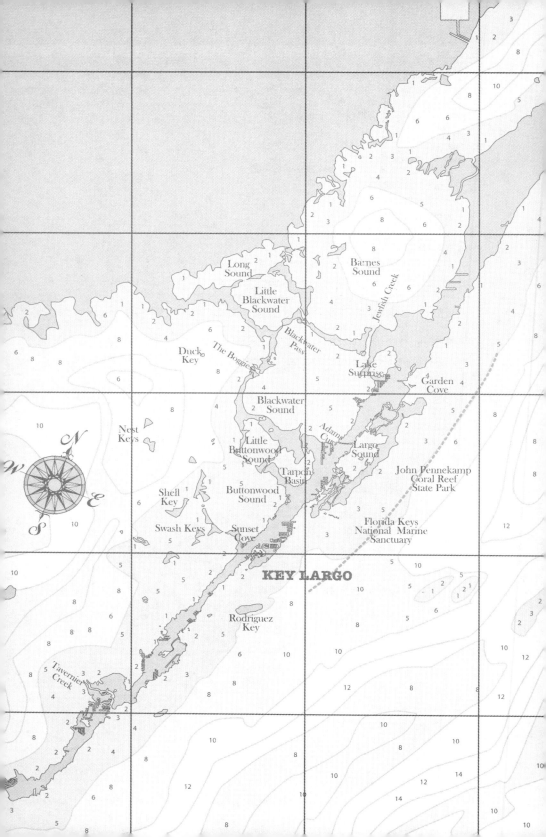

Original Harvey's Fish Sandwich

This is the original version of the Harvey's Fish Sandwich, made famous by Craig Belcher, of Craig's Restaurant in Tavernier, and previous head chef at the Pilot House Restaurant in Key Largo. Harvey Rosen cleaned fish for the Pilot House Restaurant in the 1970s. Each day, fisherman would bring their catch into the Pilot House and Harvey would fillet the fish. Through an arrangement Harvey had with the owner of the Pilot House, Ernie Bean, Harvey was allowed to keep all of the "grouper cheeks" for himself, and the rest of the fish would be sold on dinner plates at the restaurant that evening. The next morning at the Pilot House docks, as the fisherman would get ready to head out for a day on the sea, Harvey would be there serving fresh fried grouper cheek sandwiches with scrambled eggs, American cheese, and tomatoes on grilled bread. The sandwiches became a huge hit with everyone, and soon the Pilot House restaurant was serving a modified version of the Harvey's Fish Sandwich, or Super Fish Sandwich, that we know about in the Upper Keys today.

Makes 4 sandwiches

Ingredients:

- 1 pound fresh grouper (grouper cheeks are best if available)
- 1 cup all-purpose flour
- 2 cups Italian bread crumbs
- oil for frying
- 5 eggs
- 8 slices American cheese
- 1 large tomato, sliced
- 8 pieces of whole wheat bread
- 4 tablespoons butter, for grilling bread
- salt and pepper to taste

Preparation:

Pre-heat frying oil in a sauté pan until oil reaches approximately 350° F (make sure oil is hot, but do not allow it to burn). Scramble 2 eggs and set aside for "egg wash." Cut grouper fillets into 4 ounce portions or grouper "fingers" and dredge in flour, egg wash, and then in bread crumbs. Place fish in hot oil and begin to fry. Cook fish fillets for 3 to 4 minutes until fish fillets are white throughout. Remove from oil and drain on paper towels (or in true Keys cooking, place fish in a brown paper bag lined with paper towels). Begin to melt 2 tablespoons of butter in a sauté pan over medium heat for scrambling eggs. Scramble the remaining eggs and place into sauté pan. Add salt and pepper to taste, and cook scrambled eggs as usual. Remove from heat when done. Melt the remaining 2 tablespoons of butter in a very large sauté pan over medium high heat. Place sliced bread in sauté pan. Top bread slices with American cheese and sliced tomato. Grill until bread is toasted and cheese begins to melt. Top 4 slices of grilled bread with fried grouper and eggs. Place remaining grilled bread slices on top of grouper and eggs to make four sandwiches. Cut in half, serve and enjoy this little part of Keys' history!

Tuna Burger

This is another dish that I discovered in Hawaii. Made from the trimmings from tuna, as sushi chefs would prepare the tuna loins. This is a delicious way to enjoy tuna!

Makes 2 burgers

Ingredients:

¾ pound sushi-grade tuna chunks, or tuna steaks, chopped fine like ground beef
2 tablespoons Pommery mustard
2 tablespoons good quality soy sauce
½ teaspoon ginger, freshly grated
1 teaspoon chopped green scallions
1 clove garlic, chopped
1 teaspoon sesame oil
½ small yellow bell pepper, chopped
2 brioche or challah hamburger rolls
2-3 tablespoons vegetable oil
½ English cucumber, sliced thin
1 ½ cups green cabbage, shredded
2 tablespoons Key Lime Wasabi Aioli (see recipe on page 29)
salt and pepper to taste

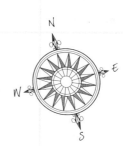

Preparation:

Place tuna, mustard, soy sauce, ginger, scallions, garlic, bell pepper, and sesame oil into a mixing bowl and mix well. Add salt and pepper to taste. Form two tuna burgers from mixture. Place a medium sauce pan on the stove over medium-high heat and add 2-3 tablespoons of vegetable oil. Heat until oil is hot. Carefully, add tuna burgers and sear for 4-5 minutes. Toast hamburger rolls while tuna burgers are cooking. Flip tuna burgers over, and cook for 4-5 minutes. Place sliced cucumbers on bottom of toasted hamburger rolls. Assemble tuna burgers on toasted rolls, and top with cabbage and Key Lime Wasabi Aioli. Kick back, and enjoy!

Blackened Shrimp Tacos with Chipotle Sour Cream and Orange Pico De Gallo

The secret to recipes that are "blackened" is the quality of the blackening spice, the higher the quality of the ingredients, the better the outcome of the dish. It is also important with any spice mixture, that you shake the container well before using, so that you do not end up with the heavier spices in the bottom of the container.

Makes 4 servings

Ingredients:

- 2 pounds fresh shrimp, approximately 16 to a pound, peeled and deveined with tails removed
- 2 ounces Sundowners' Black Caesar's Blackening Spice (recipe page 73) (or other high quality blackening spices)
- 4 tablespoons oil
- 8 soft corn or flour tortillas
- ¼ head of red or green cabbage
- ¼ bunch of cilantro, chopped
- 2 tomatoes, diced
- 1 Key lime, juiced
- 1 orange, juiced
- 1 medium yellow onion, diced
- 2 tablespoons sour cream
- 1 tablespoon chipotle peppers in adobo sauce, diced
- 2 limes

Preparation:

Lightly dust shrimp with blackening spice, being careful not to make the shrimp too spicy. Mix tomatoes, onions, and cilantro, orange and lime juice and place in a bowl for pico de gallo. Mix sour cream and chipotle peppers to taste, and set aside. Place oil in a cast-iron sauté pan and place over medium heat, and heat oil until it is very hot (but not too hot, as we don't want you to burn your house down). Add shrimp to sauté pan and cook for 2 -3 minutes per side, until shrimp are white throughout. Remove from heat immediately, so that you do not overcook the shrimp. While the shrimp are cooking, place tortillas inside a damp towel, and heat in microwave for approximately 30 seconds, to steam tortillas. Remove shrimp from the sauté pan and place inside tortillas, folded to make taco shells. Fill shells with cabbage, pico de gallo, and chipotle sour cream. Serve with extra limes and cilantro on the side.

contributed photo

Cumin Encrusted Mahi Mahi Tacos

From San Diego to Key Largo, fish tacos are showing up on menus everywhere. Flavorful, and easy to make, these tacos are universally loved. The spice cumin dates back to the Old Testament, and is the seed from the cilantro plant. Used in cooking throughout the world, cumin is especially prevalent in Mexican and Asian recipes.

Makes 4 servings

Ingredients:

- 1 ½ pounds of mahi mahi fillets, cut into fish fingers
- ¼ teaspoon granulated garlic
- ¼ teaspoon salt
- ¼ teaspoon pepper
- ½ teaspoon ground cumin
- 4 tablespoons vegetable oil
- 8 soft corn or flour tortillas
- ½ head green cabbage, shaved thin
- 2 tablespoons mayonnaise
- 1 Key lime, juiced
- 2 dashes Cholula or other hot sauce, to taste
- salt and pepper to taste

Preparation:

Mix granulated garlic, salt, pepper, and cumin, and place on a plate for encrusting mahi fingers. In a small bowl, mix cabbage, mayonnaise, lime juice, hot sauce, and salt and pepper to taste, and set aside. Place oil in a sauté pan and place over medium heat. Press fish in cumin spice mixture and place in sauté pan. Sauté fish for 2-3 minutes per side, until it is white throughout. While fish is cooking, place tortillas inside a damp towel, and heat in microwave for approximately 30 seconds, to steam tortillas. Fill tortillas with Mexican cabbage slaw, top off with cumin-encrusted fish. Fold to make tacos...eat and enjoy!

Entrées | 89

Grilled Mango Chicken Tacos with Avocado and Queso Fresco

In all of South Florida, mangos are plentiful in the summer. It's not uncommon for your neighbor to drop off 20-30 mangos at a time. So, while trying to figure out what to do with all of the mangos, we created this recipe for Señor Frijoles. Fun and flavorful barbecue chicken tacos with mango-avocado pico de gallo are a step above your typical ground beef taco.

Makes 4 servings

Ingredients:

- 4 boneless, skinless chicken breasts
- 3 mangos, peeled, pitted, and diced
- ½ cup mild barbecue sauce
- 3 tablespoons soy sauce
- 2 Key limes, juiced
- 1 small red onion, diced
- 2 tablespoons chopped fresh cilantro
- 1 Florida avocado, diced
- 1 small jalapeño, chopped
- 8 soft corn or flour tortillas, fresh are best, or steam just before using
- 2 tablespoons queso fresco, or mild feta cheese

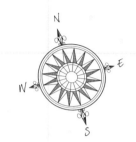

Preparation:

Place half of the mango pieces into a blender or food processor with barbecue sauce and soy sauce, and blend until mango pieces are chopped fine, and well incorporated into the barbecue sauce. Place chicken into a shallow pan, and cover with mango barbecue sauce. Place pan in refrigerator to marinate for at least 3 hours before serving. Heat a barbecue grill to medium-high. While grill is heating, combine remaining mangos, Key lime juice, diced onions, diced avocado, and fresh cilantro in a small mixing bowl. Add salt, pepper, and chopped jalapeños to taste. Set aside.

Grill chicken breasts for approximately 4 minutes per side, or until breasts are cooked throughout, being careful not to overcook. Remove chicken breasts from grill, and slice. Place sliced mango barbecue chicken inside tortillas. Top with mango-avocado pico de gallo, a sprinkle of queso fresco, and serve with extra Key lime slices and cilantro on the side.

Lobster Fajitas

One of the benefits of living in the Florida Keys is fresh lobster, and like Forrest Gump likes shrimp, we like lobster all types of ways. There's lobster bisque, and lobster fritters. Lobster Reubens and lobster scampi. Stuffed lobster, lobster tempura, lobster fried rice, lobster benedict, and lobster guacamole. Heck, what we can say? It's the price of living in paradise. So, eat like a local, and enjoy these delicious lobster fajitas from Señor Frijoles.

Makes 2 servings

Ingredients:

- 2 6-ounce lobster tails, cut into 6 pieces each
- 1 clove garlic, chopped
- ½ teaspoon onion powder
- 2 ounces butter
- 1 large yellow onion, cut in half and sliced into strips
- 1 large red or green pepper, de-seeded and sliced into strips
- 1 ounce high quality soy sauce
- 1 lime, juiced
- ¼ head iceberg lettuce, shredded
- 4 ounces cheddar cheese, shredded
- 1 medium tomato, diced
- 1 avocado, sliced
- ¼ bunch cilantro, chopped
- 2 ounces sour cream
- salt and pepper to taste
- 6 soft flour or corn tortillas

Preparation:

Place lettuce, cheddar cheese, tomato, avocado, and sour cream in separate bowls for fajita service. Place garlic, butter, onion powder and lobster in sauté pan and sauté for 4-5 minutes over medium heat until lobster is white throughout. In another sauté pan, sauté onions and peppers with salt, pepper, soy sauce, and fresh lime juice over medium heat until just wilted. Vegetables should be hot and crisp, not soft. Lobster should be white, but not overcooked.

Wrap tortillas in a lightly dampened dinner napkin and microwave for 15 to 30 seconds (to freshen and warm tortillas). When ready, use tongs to remove vegetables from sauté pan and place on serving dish. Top vegetables with freshly prepared lobster chunks, and lightly drizzle with some of the garlic butter remaining from sautéing the lobster. Fill tortillas with lobster and sautéed vegetables. Top each tortilla with lettuce, tomato, avocado, cilantro and sour cream as desired. So good! Eat immediately.

Lobster Pot Pie

The holidays always remind me of family and comfort food, so what could be better than the Keys version of a home-cooked pot pie? A Florida Keys lobster pot pie! Florida spiny lobsters are the largest export from the Florida Keys, and they are prized for their firm texture and sweet finish. This is some comfort food to remember.

Makes 4 servings

Ingredients:

¾ pound fresh Florida Keys lobster tail meat, removed from the shell
1 8" pie shell (purchase frozen from store, or make your own)
1 sheet of puff pastry (purchase from store)
1 medium Spanish onion, chopped
¼ bulb of fresh fennel, sliced thin and chopped
   (if you cannot get fennel, substitute celery)
3 tablespoons salted butter
2 cups fish stock (you can make this by boiling fish bones in water
   for 20-30 minutes, and then straining liquid)
1 cup clam juice
1 carrot diced, and boiled until soft
2 cups boiled, and diced potatoes (fresh or from a can)
1 cup frozen peas
3 tablespoons Sundowners' Black Caesar's Blackening Spice (recipe page 73)
½ cup all-purpose flour
1 egg
salt and pepper to taste

Preparation:

Cut lobster into 1-inch cubes and place lobster and 2 ½ tablespoons of blackening spice in a sauce pot full of boiling water. Allow lobster to boil in Old Bay for 3-4 minutes or until lobster is white throughout. Remove lobster from the heat immediately, strain and allow to cool. Place chopped fennel, chopped onions, and butter in a large sauté pan over medium-high heat and sauté until onions are translucent. Add the clam juice and fish stock and allow mixture to come to a boil, reduce heat to a simmer. Slowly add flour to mixture as needed to create the "juice" for the pot pie, stirring continuously. Add the remaining blackening spice to taste. Add salt and pepper to taste. Add cooked carrots, cooked diced potatoes, and frozen peas. Remove from heat. Preheat oven to 350° F. Spoon vegetable mixture into prepared pie shell. Place lobster chunks on top of vegetables. Cover pie with a sheet of puff pastry. Crimp the edges of the puff pastry to the pie shell, and remove any excess pastry as needed. Scramble the egg, and brush on top of puff pastry (this will give your pot pie a nice golden color while cooking). Cut 4-6 slits in the top of the puff pastry. Place pot pie on a baking sheet, to collect any juices that leak out during the baking process, and place in preheated oven. Bake for 40-45 minutes, or until puff pastry is golden brown and pot pie is "bubbly." Remove pie from oven, allow to cool for a few minutes, and enjoy!

Grilled Mahi Tacos with Citrus Pico de Gallo and Fresh Summer Corn

When you think of the Florida Keys, you think of seafood. And today, when you think of seafood, you think of fish tacos. Tacos have been the "food craze" of the last few years and have begun to show up on all sorts of menus, from taco trucks to fine dining establishments. Great for sharing, these fish tacos are perfect food for your next summer party.

Makes 4 servings

Ingredients:

- 1 ½ pounds of mahi mahi fillets
- 1-2 teaspoons Sundowners' Black Caesar's Blackening Spice (recipe page 73) (or other high quality blackening seasoning)
- 1-2 tablespoons oil
- 12 soft corn or flour tortillas
- ¼ head of red or green cabbage
- ¼ bunch of cilantro, chopped
- ½ jalapeño, chopped
- 2 tomatoes, diced
- 1 Key lime, juiced
- 1 Florida orange, juiced
- 1 medium yellow onion, diced
- 1 ear sweet corn kernels cut off of fresh summer corn
- salt to taste

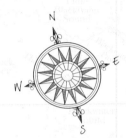

Preparation:

Mix tomatoes, onions, cilantro, jalapeño, corn kernels, Key lime juice, and orange juice to make pico de gallo. Season pico with salt to taste, and set aside. Lightly dust fresh fish fillets with blackening seasoning to taste, sprinkle with oil, and cook over a preheated barbecue grill on medium high heat. Cook fish for 2-3 minutes per side, or until fish is white throughout, being careful not to overcook fish. While fish is cooking, place tortillas inside a damp towel, and heat in microwave for approximately 30 seconds, to steam tortillas. Remove fish from grill and place inside tortillas, folded to make taco shells. Fill shells with cabbage, pico de gallo, and fresh corn.

Soft Corn Taco Shells
("Not your regular corn tortillas")

So these soft corn taco shells are made the same way you would make flour tortillas, but with cornmeal added for additional flavor and texture. Unlike regular corn tortillas, these tortillas are great for tacos since the gluten in the flour will allow the tortillas to be bent without breaking.

Ingredients:

- 1 ½ cups fine ground cornmeal
- 3 cups all-purpose flour
- 1 teaspoon salt
- 2 eggs
- 4 cups water

Preparation:

Place all ingredients into a large mixing bowl and mix well.

Preheat a seasoned (lightly buttered) non-stick skillet over high heat. Pour approximately ¾ cup of the tortilla mixture into the center of the skillet and shake so that tortilla is as thin as possible. When the edges begin to curl, shake the tortilla loose (you may need to use a spatula to help you do this). Flip the tortilla and cook for 20-30 more seconds. Place tortilla into layered paper towels to keep them from sticking and place into the oven to keep warm.

Grilled Chicken Tacos with Avocado and Corn Salsa

Ingredients:

   2-3 large chicken breasts
   2 oranges, juiced
   3 Key limes, juice 2 for the chicken marinade.
   2 ounces soy sauce
   1 tablespoon blackening spic
   1 Haas avocado, ripe
   3 ears of corn
   1 small tomato, diced
   ½ jalapeno pepper, seeds removed and diced
   ½ bunch cilantro
   4 tablespoons prepared black beans, rinsed
   salt and pepper to taste
   8 soft corn taco shells (see recipe on facing page) or
   8 soft flour tortillas (homemade or store bought)

Preparation:

Marinate chicken breasts in orange juice, juice from 2 key limes and soy sauce for 6 to 8 hours. Preheat barbecue grille. Grill ears of corn and allow ears to cool. Cut corn off the cobs and place into a bowl. Add tomatoes, jalapeno peppers, black beans, to the grilled corn kernels and mix well. Add salt and pepper to taste. Season with the juice from the remaining key lime. Remove chicken breasts from marinade and pat dry. Sprinkle chicken breast with blackening spice and grill until chicken breast is cooked throughout. Allow chicken breast to rest for 4-5 minutes, then slice chicken breasts into strips. Slice avocado just before using. Place chicken breast slices into warm tortilla shells and top with fresh avocado slices and corn salsa. Garnish with cilantro leaves, serve and enjoy!

Lobster Tacos with Cabbage Slaw and Avocado Cream

Lobster tacos? Crazy, I know! Your family is going to love them.

Makes 8 tacos

Ingredients:

- 2 6-8 ounce Florida lobster tails, remove meat and cut into chunks
- 8 6 inch corn or flour tortillas
- 1 small jar sliced pickled jalapeño peppers
- ¼ bunch cilantro
- ¼ head of white cabbage, shredded
- 1 avocado, smashed
- 3 tablespoons sour cream
- 3 Key limes, juiced
- 1 egg
- 2 cups all-purpose flour
- 1 cup ice cold water
- 2-3 tablespoons olive oil
- 2-3 tablespoons apple cider vinegar
- vegetable or corn oil for frying

Preparation:

Prepare avocado cream by mixing avocado, sour cream, and 1 tablespoon lime juice. Mix well, until cream is smooth. Refrigerate.

Toss white cabbage with olive oil, apple cider vinegar, remaining lime juice, and salt and pepper to taste. Cabbage slaw should be coated with oil and vinegar, but not "watery." Heat oil for frying. Oil should be approximately 350° F. Prepare tempura batter by mixing 1 cup flour and 1 cup ice cold water, mix well, but do not over beat. Add 1 egg to batter and mix again. Dredge lobster chunks in remaining flour, then into tempura batter. Carefully place battered lobster chunks into frying oil. Fry for 3-4 minutes until lobster chunks are white throughout.

While lobster chunks are cooking, wrap tortillas in a clean, damp kitchen towel and steam in microwave for 20-30 seconds, or until warm. Remove lobster chunks from fryer and drain on paper towels. Fill warmed tortillas with cabbage slaw, lobster chunks, avocado cream, picked jalapeño rings, and fresh cilantro.

Onion Encrusted Lobster with Key Lime Butter

This is one of my all-time favorite recipes for lobster! The onion crust is great on shrimp, scallops, or chicken, but on lobster it is amazing. Try this lobster dish the next time you have company in town, and let me know what you think.

Makes 4 servings

Ingredients:

4 6-8 ounce lobster tails - butterfly lobster tails and remove the meat from the shell
1 large yellow onion, sliced thin for onion rings
½ cup panko bread crumbs
1 ½ cups flour
1 tablespoon Sundowners' Black Caesar's Blackening Spice (recipe page 73)
2 eggs, beaten
vegetable oil for frying

Preparation:

In a large, deep sauté pan or fryer, preheat enough vegetable oil to cover onions. Heat oil to approximately 350° F. In a medium bowl place 1 cup flour and blackening spice. Toss sliced onions in flour mixture and lightly shake off any excess flour. Place dusted onion rings into hot oil, and fry for 4-5 minutes, stirring onions occasionally, until onions are dark brown. Remove onions from the oil, and place on paper towels to remove any excess oil. Allow onion rings to cool to room temperature. Then using a kitchen knife or a food processor, chop onion rings until they are about the size of the panko bread crumbs. Place chopped onion rings and panko bread crumbs into a medium bowl, and mix well. Dredge lobster tails through remaining flour, then through the beaten eggs, and then press lobster tail into the onion ring and panko bread crumb mixture. Place a large sauté pan on the stove and add enough oil to just coat the bottom of the pan. Place battered lobster tails into the sauté pan and sauté over medium high heat for 3-4 minutes per side, or until onion crust is lightly browned. Remove sauté pan from the stove and place into an oven preheated to 350° F, until lobster tails are white throughout. Approximately 10 minutes. Remove lobster tails from oven. Top with Key lime butter and enjoy!

Key Lime Butter

(prepare in advance)

6 Key limes, juiced
1 stick of butter
¼ cup of good quality dry white wine

Preparation:

Melt butter over medium heat, add dry white wine, and Key lime juice. Remove from heat and let rest at room temperature.

Roasted Tomato Salsa

Ingredients:

    2 medium vine ripe tomatoes cut in half
    1 small Spanish onion, peeled and cut into thick slices
    ¼ jalapeño
    1 garlic clove, chopped
    ¼ bunch of cilantro
    pinch of salt and pepper
    2 Key limes
    2-3 tablespoons olive oil

Preparation:

Preheat barbecue to medium high. Brush tomato halves, onion slices, and jalapeño with olive oil and place on barbecue grill. Grill for 3 to 5 minutes per side. Remove from grill and allow vegetables to cool. Chop vegetables by hand, and mix with garlic, cilantro, salt and pepper. Cut Key limes and squeeze over salsa to taste. Enjoy!

Sundowners' Tartar Sauce

Great for fish sandwiches or as a dip for avocados or artichokes.

Ingredients:

    1 cup good quality mayonnaise
    1 teaspoon minced garlic
    1 lemon, juiced
    Dash Worcestershire
    2 Tablespoon French mustard
    1 Tablespoon chopped dill relish
    2 Tablespoons chopped parsley
    1 Tablespoon scallions, chopped
    Salt and Pepper to taste

Preparation:

Mix and keep refrigerated.

Corn Meal Fried Oysters with Mango Salsa

These oysters from Marker 88 are fresh tasting and beautiful to look at. A sure crowd pleaser and easy to make. If ripe mangos are not available, you can also try these fried oysters with the Remoulade recipe on page 37.

Makes 24-30 oysters

Ingredients:

30 fresh oysters, shucked, drained & cleaned (clean shells and save for later)
1 ¼ cups yellow corn meal
½ cup all-purpose flour
2 eggs, lightly beaten
1 ½ cups milk
¼ cup melted butter
1 tablespoon baking powder
½ teaspoon salt
2 ½ cups vegetable oil for frying
Key lime wedges for garnish

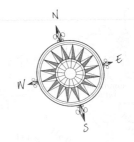

Preparation:

In a medium bowl, combine corn meal, flour, eggs, milk, butter, baking powder, and salt. Stir until batter is smooth. In a large sauce pan or deep fryer, preheat oil to 350° F, or until oil is hot. Do not let oil begin to burn. Dredge each oyster in batter and fry in batches until golden brown, approximately one to two minutes. Remove oysters from frying oil with a slotted spoon and drain on paper towels. Place 1 teaspoon mango puree into each oyster shell. Top mango puree with one fried oyster, and top each fried oyster with one teaspoon of mango salsa. Serve immediately, while the oysters are still warm.

Mango Salsa

Great for grilled or blackened fish, this salsa is also excellent on fried oysters.

Makes 2-3 servings (or enough for 20-30 oysters)

Ingredients:

1 medium ripe mango, cut into ¼ inch cubes
2 medium red onions, diced
2 teaspoons fresh cilantro, chopped
1 large tomato, diced
1 jalapeño, chopped
2 Key limes (or 1 Persian lime) juiced
salt to taste

Preparation:

Place all ingredients into a bowl, mix and set aside.

Butter Baked Lionfish with Fresh Vegetables

Since lionfish have no natural predators in the Atlantic, the Bahamas decided to put together a list of recipes to combat lionfish in Bahamian waters, thus making lionfish part of the local food chain. Lionfish spines are venomous and should be handled with caution during the cleaning process, but once cleaned, lionfish fillets are safe and flavorful, a clean white fish.

Makes 2 servings

Ingredients:

16 ounces of lionfish fillets (or other white fish)
4 ounces of butter (cut into small cubes)
¼ Spanish onion, sliced
½ yellow squash, sliced thin
½ zucchini sliced thin
1 carrot cut into ¼ inch sticks
    (like you would use for garnish with chicken wings)
2 dinner rolls
2 Key limes
salt and pepper to taste

aluminum foil (for cooking fish in)

Preparation:

To clean the lionfish, use heavy rubber gloves and kitchen scissors to trim off all lionfish fins at their base. Once the fins are removed, you can fillet the lionfish like any other bottom fish. Tear off 2 pieces of foil large enough to place fish fillets in. Turn on barbecue grill to preheat on high and close lid. Place 8 ounces of fish in each piece of foil. Top each fillet with onion, squash, and zucchini slices. Place carrot sticks on each side of fish. Add salt and pepper to taste. Place small cubes of butter on top of fish, and squeeze Key limes over both fish fillets. Fold up foil to make sealed foil pouches and place on barbecue grill. Close lid, and cook for approximately 7 minutes until fish fillets are white throughout. Remove and serve! Use dinner rolls to soak up the juices in the foil packs.

You can also do this in an oven preheated to 500° F.

Simple Grilled Fish with Yellow Rice and Peas

Easy and delicious. What more can be said about simple grilled fish... except that it goes great with a Sauvignon Blanc or nice Chardonnay.

Makes 4 servings

Ingredients:

- 2 pounds fresh mahi mahi or grouper fillets cut into 8-ounce portions
- 2 tablespoons coarse sea salt
- 1 tablespoon black pepper
- 1 teaspoon fresh garlic, chopped
- 2 cups Italian salad dressing (prepared fresh or out of a jar)
- 3 Key limes cut into wedges
- 1 package of yellow rice, prepared
- 1 small can of peas, add to yellow rice as you remove the rice from heat

Preparation:

Dust both sides of fillets with salt, pepper, and garlic. Brush liberally with Italian dressing. Place fish on a hot, oiled barbecue grill, and grill until the fillet is white throughout. Do not overcook. Serve fish with yellow rice and fresh Key lime wedges on the side.

Fried Ballyhoo... you can eat them!

Who knew you could eat them! They are a surprisingly good snack. Fried whole with the scales and innards removed, you eat the bones and all (except for the backbone), or use a fork to flake off the meat.

Ingredients:

6 small-to-medium fresh ballyhoo
1 cup flour
1 egg
3 tablespoons milk
salt and pepper to taste
oil for frying.

Preparation:

Preheat the oil to approximately 350° F. Cut the heads off the ballyhoo, remove their innards, and using a butter knife, scale the ballyhoo (your fish market should be able to do this for you). Mix egg and milk well. Season flour with salt and pepper. Dust ballyhoo with flour, then dredge in egg, and lightly dust ballyhoo again with flour. Carefully place ballyhoo in oil and fry for 3-5 minutes, or until ballyhoo are 145° F, or flaky throughout. Serve warm and enjoy!

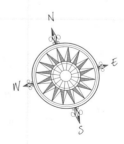

Ballyhoo's Pan Fried Hog Fish with Conch Salad Salsa

No food says "the Florida Keys" more than conch salad and hog fish, and Ballyhoo's has put the two together in this amazing recipe. Make your own conch salad or you can purchase conch salad from Key Largo Fisheries in Key Largo or from Keys Fisheries in Marathon. Of course you can pick up your fresh hog fish from either of the fisheries while you are there as well!

Makes 4 servings

Ingredients:

 4 6-ounce hog fish fillets
  (note: if hog fish is not available, you can use any fresh snapper)
 2 cups panko Japanese bread crumbs
 2 eggs, whisked for egg wash
 1 cup of flour
 salt and pepper to taste
 ½ cup vegetable oil for pan frying
 1 pint prepared conch salad
 Key lime butter - see page 97

Preparation:

Dredge hog fish in flour, then in egg wash, and then press in panko bread crumbs seasoned with salt and pepper. Place vegetable oil into a medium sauté pan and place on stove over medium high heat. Oil should be hot, but not too hot. Place hog fish fillets in pan and cook for 3 to 4 minutes per side. Fish should be white and flaky throughout. Do not overcook. Remove fish from pan, top each fillet with 3 tablespoons of conch salad, and drizzle with Key lime butter. Enjoy!

Mojo Marinade
(can be prepared 3-4 days in advance)

Ingredients:

1 ½ cups fresh orange juice
1 cup Spanish olive oil
½ cup fresh lemon juice
½ cup fresh Key lime juice
    (or Persian lime juice, if Key limes are not available)
4 heads of garlic
1 medium yellow onion, chopped fine
2 teaspoons oregano
2 teaspoons basil
1 teaspoon cumin
2 teaspoons of salt
1 teaspoon cracked black pepper

Preparation:

Prepare the mojo marinade by mashing the garlic, salt, and black pepper in a mortar or food processor. Stir in the juices and allow mixture to sit for at least 30 minutes. In a sauce pan, heat the oil, basil, oregano, cumin and chopped onions over medium heat until the onions become soft. Remove oil from heat, cool, and add to juice mixture. Refrigerate mojo marinade after making.

"Betsy the Lobster" is a famous Islamorada landmark, found at the Rain Barrel, mile marker 87.

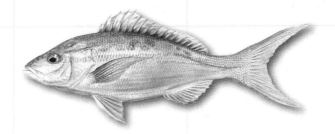

Mojo Marinated Whole Fried Yellowtail Snapper

Whole pan fried fish is a Cuban favorite and a specialty of Sundowners. Mojo marinated, dusted and floured, pan fried, then topped with a drizzle of garlic butter... the taste is amazing!

Makes 4 servings

Ingredients:

    3-4 cups mojo marinade, see recipe on page 104
    4 one-to-two-pound whole yellowtail, gutted and descaled
        (the fish market can do this for you)
    3 cups vegetable oil for pan frying
    2 cups all-purpose flour
    6-8 tablespoons butter
    3 tablespoons chopped garlic
    3 Key limes, juiced
    2 ounces dry white wine

Preparation:

Check your whole yellowtails to make sure that all scales have been removed and rinse yellowtails in fresh water. Place 3 slits on both sides of each yellowtail, cutting through the skin, so the marinade can soak into the fish, and place whole yellowtails into a heavy duty bag or bowl for marinating. Add mojo marinade to the bag and mix well to coat the fish. Allow fish to marinate for at least 2 hours.

Remove fish from marinade and wipe off excess. Dust both sides of fish with flour. (Preheat oven to 350° F, and turn off heat.) Place a large sauté pan on the stove over medium high heat. Add oil and allow the oil to get hot (approximately 350° F). Place whole fish into the oil, and cook until the fish is flaky throughout (approximately 4 minutes per side).

Place cooked fish onto a pan lined with paper towels and place in the warm oven (oven off) to keep fish warm while the rest of the fish are cooking. In a small sauté pan, over medium heat, add butter, chopped garlic, lime juice, and white wine. Sauté until garlic begins to brown, then remove from heat. Once all fish have been pan fried, plate fish and drizzle with garlic butter.

Grilled Corn with Tomatoes, Roasted Jalapeños, and Fresh Cilantro

Makes 4 servings

Ingredients:

- 4 large cobs of fresh sweet corn
- 1 jalapeño
- 2 tablespoons vegetable oil
- 1 large tomato, diced
- 1 clove garlic, chopped
- 2 tablespoons butter
- 2-3 tablespoons cilantro, chopped

Preparation:

Pre-heat barbecue grill. Lightly brush corn cobs and jalapeño with vegetable oil, and place both on the barbecue grill. Cook corn for 2-3 minutes per side. You want the smokiness of the grill, so grill marks on the corn are a good thing. Once corn is done, remove from the grill and allow to cool. Remove jalapeño from the grill once it becomes soft, and set aside to cool. Cut corn kernels off of cooled cobs, and coarsely chop roasted jalapeño. Remember to remove the jalapeño seeds if you prefer less heat. Add corn kernels and jalapeño to the sauté pan and sauté for 3-4 minutes, or until corn is hot throughout, stirring occasionally. Add diced tomatoes to sauté pan, stir, and remove pan from heat. Add salt and pepper to taste. Top with fresh chopped cilantro and serve.

Amaretto Mashed Sweet Potatoes with Marshmallows

Makes 6 Servings

Ingredients:

2 ¼ lb. sweet potatoes (peeled and boiled)
2 cups milk
3 tablespoons brown sugar
3 tablespoons melted butter
½ teaspoon salt
1 dash white pepper
1 dash cinnamon
1 bag small marshmallows
1 ½ ounces Lazzaroni Amaretto

Preparation:

Set 2 cups of marshmallows aside. Place the remaining marshmallows, Amaretto, brown sugar and butter into a medium sauté pan on stove. Mix constantly and adjust heat accordingly, being careful not to burn. Mash sweet potatoes with an electric beater. Slowly add milk to mashed sweet potatoes, then mix in Amaretto butter. Spoon mixture into a buttered casserole dish. Top with additional marshmallows, cover, and bake in 250 degree oven for approximately 20 minutes, or until marshmallows have melted.

Melody Guy performs at one of the Key Largo Original Music Fests.

Lightly Blackened Yellowtail Snapper with Mango Salsa

This is a great way to enjoy yellowtail snapper or any light and flaky fish. The spiciness of the blackening is tempered by the sweetness of the mango salsa.

Makes 4 servings

Ingredients:

- 1 ½ - 2 pounds of Yellowtail snapper fillets (or other light white fish)
- 3 ounces of Sundowners' Black Caesar's Blackening Spice (recipe page 73) (or other high quality blackening spices)
- 4 ounces unsalted butter
- 2 ounces dry white wine
- 1 ripe mango, diced
- 1 green pepper, diced
- 1 tomato, diced
- ½ red onion, diced
- 4 fresh Key limes, juiced
- Salt and pepper to taste

Preparation:

In a bowl, add diced mango, green peppers, diced tomatoes, red onions, Key lime juice, and salt and pepper, and mix well. Cut yellowtail fillets into a least 4 pieces and make sure that all pin bones have been removed. Lightly dust both sides of snapper fillets with blackening seasoning. The idea for this dish is to have a snapper that is lightly blackened, so be careful with the blackening spices. Set prepared fish fillets aside. Begin to heat a cast iron skillet on the stove over medium high heat (or other heavy sauté pan if a cast iron pan is not available). Add 3 ounces of butter to skillet and stir until butter has melted and begins to turn brown. In another sauté pan, add 1 ounce butter and white wine, and place on stove over medium heat. Add fish fillets to cast iron skillet and cook for 2 -3 minutes per side, or until fillets are just white throughout. Remove fish from heat and set aside. Add mango salsa to butter and wine mixture and sauté for 2 – 3 minutes until diced mango chunks just begin to turn soft. Remove warm salsa from heat and spoon over fish. Amazing!

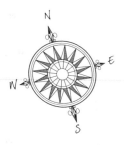

Ginger Grilled Tuna with Pineapple Ponzu

This recipe is a twist on Sundowners Ginger Steamed Grouper with Pineapple Ponzu made with fresh ahi tuna, and ground ginger.

Makes 4 servings

Ingredients:

- 2 pounds ahi grade tuna fillets, cut into 8 ounce portions
- 2 tablespoons ground ginger
- 2 tablespoons coarse sea salt
- 1 tablespoon black pepper
- 2 tablespoons Sundowners' Black Caesar's Blackening Spice (recipe page 73)
- 4 servings sticky rice (prepared)
- 1 pound fresh baby spinach, blanched just before serving
- 2 cups pineapple ponzu sauce (see below)
- 2 tablespoons diced scallions

Preparation:

Place ginger, sea salt, black pepper, and blackening spice into a bowl and mix well. Dust both sides of tuna fillets with spice mixture, holding back a tablespoon of the mixture to season the spinach. Place fish on a hot, oiled barbecue grill, and grill until the tuna is cooked to temperature (I recommend rare to medium rare). Place rice in the center of a large bowl and surround it with hot spinach. Season hot spinach with the remainder of the ginger spice mixture. Set cooked fish on top of rice in the center of the bowl and ladle ponzu over top of the fish, creating a small puddle of ponzu in the bottom of the bowl. Top the fish with diced scallions and enjoy.

Pineapple Ponzu Sauce

Ingredients:

- 1 cup rice vinegar
- 1 ½ cups low-sodium soy sauce
- ¾ cup fresh Key lime juice
- ¾ cup pineapple juice

Preparation:

Mix all ingredients together and let sit.

Island Style Fish Poached in Coconut Milk

Cooking in coconut milk has long been a staple of Thai and Brazilian cuisines, and has made it to the Keys by way of Key Largo. This dish is sweet and spicy and perfectly complements the flavor of mahi mahi. It is very easy to make at home.

Makes 2 servings

Ingredients:

1 pound fish fillets (mahi mahi or mild white fish),
    skin removed, cut into 8 ounce portions
1 teaspoon fresh chopped ginger
1 teaspoon chopped garlic
6 fresh basil leaves
1 tablespoon Thai sweet chili sauce (add more if you like this dish hotter)
6 ounces unsweetened coconut milk
3 ounces cream or milk
3 teaspoons vegetable oil
2 tablespoons toasted sliced almonds
1 tablespoon toasted coconut

Preparation:

Place oil in sauté pan over medium heat. Once oil is hot, add chopped ginger and garlic. Sauté until ginger and garlic become brown. Add Thai sweet chili sauce, fresh fish fillets, milk, and coconut milk. Top fish with chopped basil leaves and cover. Poach for 5 minutes. Turn fish over, cover again and poach for an additional 3 minutes (or until fish is white throughout). Remove from heat and serve. Serve with sticky coconut rice and fresh steamed vegetables.

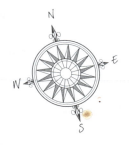

Sticky Coconut Rice

This rice goes great with any dish containing fruits, fruit salsas, or coconut. Try this with the lightly blackened yellowtail with mango salsa, or with the coconut poached fish above.

Makes 6-8 servings

Ingredients:

- 2 cups jasmine rice
- 2 cups coconut milk
- 1 ¾ cups water
- ½ teaspoon salt
- ½ tablespoon butter
- 4 heaping tablespoons shredded coconut, toasted

Preparation:

For this recipe, you will need a medium-sized pot with a tight fighting lid. Place all ingredients, except toasted shredded coconut, into a medium-sized pot and place on the stove over medium-high heat. Stirring occasionally, allow mixture to come to a boil. Cover pot and reduce heat to low. Allow rice to simmer for 15-20 minutes, until most of the liquid has been absorbed by the rice. Keep rice covered and remove from heat. Allow rice to continue cooking for 10-15 more minutes. Flake with a fork or chopsticks, and spoon rice onto plates and top with toasted shredded coconut.

Grouper Martinique with Tomato Basil Concasse and Bananas

Makes 4 servings

Ingredients:
- 2 pounds grouper fillets, cut into individual portions (or other white fish)
- 3 eggs
- ¼ cup milk
- ¼ cup of extra virgin olive oil
- 4 tablespoons butter
- 2 whole, ripe bananas
- ¼ cup white wine
- 5 fresh Key limes, juiced
- Tomato Basil Concasse (see below, prepare first)

Preparation:

Crack eggs and milk into a bowl large enough to dredge fish in, and mix well to create egg wash for the fish. Add olive oil to a large sauté pan and place over medium high heat. Dredge fish through egg wash and place into hot oil. Sauté fish for 2-3 minutes per side, and remove fish from sauté pan when fish is white throughout, being careful not to overcook. Wipe out sauté pan and return to stove. Add butter. Once butter is melted add peeled ripe bananas cut into quarters, and sauté bananas until warm throughout, approximately 3 minutes. Remove bananas from pan, add white wine and lemon juice and reduce by half. Place fish fillets on plates, top with sautéed bananas, tomato basil concasse, and finish with lemon butter from sauté pan. Serve and enjoy.

Tomato Basil Concasse

Ingredients:

- ½ cup of chopped onions
- 2 cloves of garlic, minced
- 1 tablespoon olive oil
- 3 large tomatoes, diced
- ½ tablespoon sugar
- 2 bay leaves
- 2 tablespoons fresh, chopped basil
- 1 teaspoon fresh, chopped rosemary
- 1 teaspoon fresh, chopped thyme
- 1 teaspoon fresh, chopped oregano
- salt and pepper to taste

Preparation:

Place olive oil, onions and garlic into a medium sauté pan and sauté over medium heat until soft. Add tomatoes, herbs, and seasonings and simmer for 15 minutes, stirring occasionally. Remove bay leaves and set aside.

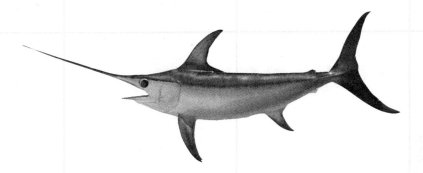

Swordfish Mediterranean

Swordfish is a delicious steak fish that is amazing on the grill. Once thought to be over fished commercially, this fish has made quite a comeback off the waters of the Florida Keys, as a day boat, line caught fish. Below is one of the grilled swordfish recipes that we serve at Marker 88, so give it a try, and enjoy!

Makes 4 servings

Ingredients:

- 4 6-ounce swordfish fillets
- ½ cup olive oil
- 2 cloves of garlic, chopped
- 2 tablespoons fresh basil, chopped
- 2 tablespoons fresh mint, chopped
- 4-5 Key limes, juiced
- 3 tablespoons decent quality Feta cheese, crumbled
- salt and pepper to taste

Preparation:

In a bowl, mix olive oil, garlic, basil, mint, and Key lime juice. Lightly season the swordfish fillets with salt and pepper to taste. Brush swordfish fillets with Key lime oil mixture and place on the barbecue grill. Grill fillets for 3-4 minutes per side, or until fillets are just white throughout. Be careful not to overcook. Remove fillets from grill. Top fillets with Key lime oil mixture and sprinkle with Feta cheese.

Entrées

Andrew Lewis of Boca Raton holds up a beautiful dolphin.

Mojo Mahi Bites

Key Largo Fisheries is the premier fish packing house in the Upper Keys. Started by Jack and Dottie Hill in 1972, Key Largo Fisheries is known for their fresh and frozen seafood, which is shipped to restaurants, stores, and families throughout the world. At the recent Key Largo Stone Crab and Seafood Fest, Key Largo Fisheries was the premier sponsor and operator of the seafood tent, where their mojo marinated mahi bites were the talk of the festival. These fish fingers are moist and flaky with just a hint of citrus. Try them today!

Makes 6 servings

Ingredients:

    3 pounds of mahi fillets, cleaned of the blood line and cut into fingers
    3 cups of Italian bread crumbs
    oil for frying

Mojo Marinade

(can be prepared 3-4 days in advance)

    1 ½ cups fresh orange juice
    1 cup Spanish olive oil
    ½ cup fresh lemon juice
    ½ cup fresh Key lime juice (or Persian lime juice)
    4 heads of garlic
    1 medium yellow onion, chopped fine
    2 teaspoons oregano
    2 teaspoons basil
    1 teaspoon cumin
    2 teaspoons of salt
    1 teaspoon cracked black pepper

Preparation:

Prepare the mojo marinade by mashing the garlic, salt, and black pepper in a mortar or food processor. Stir in the juice; allow mixture to sit for at least 30 minutes. In a sauce pan, heat the oil, basil, oregano, cumin and chopped onions over medium heat until the onions become soft. Remove oil from heat, cool, and add to juice mixture. Refrigerate mojo marinade after making. Add mahi fingers to mojo marinade and allow the fingers to marinate in the refrigerator for a minimum of 30 minutes. Remove mahi fingers from mojo and dredge in bread crumbs. Allow battered fish fillets to "rest" for 30 minutes before frying, so the batter can "set." Heat frying oil in sauté pan on medium high heat until oil is approximately 350° F (make sure oil is hot, but do not allow it to burn). Place fish fingers in oil and cook for 3-4 minutes, until fish fingers are white and flaky throughout. Remove fingers from oil and drain on paper towels (a brown paper bag, lined with paper towels works great for this). Serve fish fingers with Key limes and tartar sauce!

Blackwater Pasta

A Sundowners original. Loaded with shrimp, chicken, smoky pancetta, fresh baby greens, and a hint of heat from the red pepper flakes, this dish is quickly becoming a favorite.

Makes 4 servings

Ingredients:

- 1 pound shrimp, peeled and deveined
- 1 ½ pound skinless chicken breasts, cut into strips
- 6 ounces pancetta cut into strips
- 1 pound penne pasta
- 3 tomatoes, diced
- 4 cups baby greens (or baby spinach if you prefer)
- 3 cloves garlic, chopped
- ½ cup white wine
- 4 tablespoons butter
- 2 ounces olive oil
- 4 tablespoons grated Parmesan cheese
- 1 ½ teaspoons red pepper flakes
- salt to taste

Preparation:

In a large pot, begin to boil water for pasta. In a large sauté pan, add oil, garlic, and pancetta strips over medium heat until edges of pancetta begin to turn brown and crispy. Add pasta to boiling water and begin to cook until al dente (see instructions on package, should take approximately 12 minutes). Add chicken to sauté pan and sauté for 3-5 minutes, until chicken is light pink in center. Add white wine and shrimp and sauté for 3-5 minutes until shrimp are almost white throughout. Add butter and red pepper flakes, reduce and stir. Strain pasta. In a large bowl, place baby greens, hot pasta, and contents of sauté pan. Toss well and top with Parmesan cheese

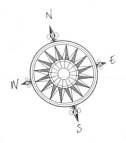

Sundowners' Key Lime Seafood

One of the most popular dishes at restaurants throughout Key Largo, is seafood sautéed with fresh Key Lime juice, Tabasco, garlic butter, tomatoes and scallions, and served over penne or rice. The following is Sundowners version of the dish.

Makes 4 servings

Ingredients:

20 large shrimp, peeled and deveined with the tails removed
2 fresh Florida lobster tails, removed from their shells, and cut into large chunks
½ pound jumbo lump crab meat
2 tomatoes, diced
6 scallions, diced
6-8 fresh Key limes, juiced
4 tablespoons lightly salted butter
5 dashes Tabasco sauce (add more or less to taste)
2 ounces white wine
4 cloves fresh garlic, chopped
1 pound penne pasta (or 2 cups of uncooked rice, prepared)
Fresh grated Parmesan cheese
salt and pepper to taste

Preparation:

In a large pot, begin to boil water for pasta. In a large sauté pan, add butter, garlic, Key lime juice (to taste), white wine and Tabasco sauce, and stir over medium heat until butter has melted. Add pasta to boiling water and begin to cook until al dente (see instructions on package, should take approximately 12 minutes). Add lobster tail to butter mixture and sauté for 3-4 minutes until lobster chunks have begun to turn white. Add shrimp and tomatoes and sauté until shrimp and lobster are just done. Add salt and pepper to taste. Do not overcook. Add jumbo lump crab and scallions, stir gently so as to not break up the jumbo lump crab pieces, and remove from heat. Strain pasta. In a large bowl, place hot pasta, and contents of sauté pan. Toss well and top with Parmesan cheese.

Key West Pink Shrimp, Chicken and Sausage Gumbo

During the recent Key Largo Food and Wine Festival, the Sauce Boss was in Key Largo singing about New Orleans, and cooking up a mean gumbo. The gumbo was a huge hit, and customers were asking for a gumbo recipe, so for all you gumbo lovers, here's a recipe from my collection that I think does gumbo justice.

Makes 8 - 10 Servings

Ingredients:

- 2 pounds (sized 26 to 30 a pound) Key West pink shrimp, peeled and deveined (for seafood gumbo reduce the shrimp and add oysters or crab meat)
- 1 pound andouille sausage, cut into ½ inch slices (if andouille sausage is not available, substitute cubes of smoked ham)
- 3-4 pounds of skin-on chicken with bones (a whole small chicken works great for this, but chicken quarters also work well)
- 4 green onions, chopped
- ½ cup unsalted butter
- 1 cup flour
- 3 tablespoons gumbo filé (optional. This should definitely be used, if you are planning on leaving the okra out of the recipe.)
- 2 tablespoons vegetable oil
- 1 medium onion, chopped
- 1 bell pepper, seeds removed and chopped
- 2 stalks celery, chopped
- 4 garlic cloves, chopped
- 3 bay leaves
- 2 medium zucchinis, chopped
- 1 pound okra (fresh is best, frozen is okay) chopped
- 3 tablespoons Sundowners' Black Caesar's Blackening Spice (recipe page 73) (or other high quality blackening spice)
- 1 tablespoon Old Bay or Zatarain's seasoning
- ½ ounce Tabasco Habanero Hot Sauce (add more if you like it spicier)
- 8 cups prepared white rice (keep warm)

Entrées | 119

Bill Wharton (The Sauce Boss) has cooked gumbo on stage for over 175,000 for free. He mixes his own spicy original music—Florida Slide Guitar Blues—and adds his famous Liquid Summer hot sauce right into every night's cooking demonstration of his own gumbo recipe. It's a multi-sensory, soul-shouting picnic of rock and roll brotherhood. And at the end of the night, everybody eats. Here he is shown performing at Sundowners during Key Largo's Food and Wine Festival. *Photo by Kathy Romano.*

Preparation:

Place chicken in a large stock pot. Cover chicken completely with water and place on stove to boil. Remove chicken from water when completely cooked through to cool. Reserve 8 cups of chicken stock for gumbo, and discard remaining. When chicken is cool, pull chicken meat from the bones and set meat aside. Make a roux by melting butter in a large cast iron skillet over medium-low heat. Slowly whisk in the flour stirring constantly over low heat until the roux is the color of a dark copper penny, about 25 – 30 minutes. If the roux burns at all discard, as this is one of the major flavor components of this dish. Remove roux from heat. Mix the gumbo filé and 1 cup of the chicken stock together until smooth. In a large stock pot, place vegetable oil, onions, celery, bell pepper, and garlic and sauté over medium-high heat until soft. Reduce heat to simmer and add roux, remaining chicken stock, bay leaves, and gumbo filé/stock mix to stock pot. Add blackening spice, seafood boil, Tabasco, andouille sausage, okra, zucchini, and pulled chicken and simmer for 2 -3 hours, stirring occasionally. Add shrimp and simmer for approximately 20 minutes, or until shrimp are white throughout, stirring occasionally. Serve gumbo over white rice, sprinkle with green onions.

Note: If using gumbo filé, do not allow gumbo to come to a boil, as the gumbo may become "stringy."

Bouillabaisse

This is a hearty seafood soup, served over toasted sourdough bread cubes, that packs tons of flavor.

Make 4 servings

Ingredients:

BROTH

    8 cups fish stock (chicken stock, either homemade or prepared from bouillon cubes, can be substituted)
    1 small Spanish onion, diced small
    1 green pepper, diced small
    4 stalks celery, diced small
    2 tablespoons minced garlic
    1 tablespoon olive oil
    1 ½ teaspoon cumin
    1 ½ teaspoon fennel seed
    1 ½ teaspoon sage
    1 ½ teaspoon coriander
    3 bay leaves
    4 teaspoon oregano
    4 teaspoon basil
    1/4 teaspoon cayenne
    2 cups crushed tomatoes in puree
    ½ cup white wine

    -sourdough bread cubes-

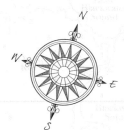

SEAFOOD

    12 large shrimp, peeled and deveined
    16 small clams
    16 mussels
    16 scallops
    1 pound mild fish (snapper, cod) cut into 1-inch cubes

Preparation:

Prepare fish stock. Reserve.

Sauté onion, pepper, celery, garlic and olive oil over medium heat until vegetables soften. Add herbs and spices to the pan and cook for 2 minutes. Add white wine and crushed tomatoes and simmer 5 minutes.

Combine fish stock with vegetable mixture in a stock pot or large sauce pan (min. 1 gallon capacity) and simmer for 1 hour. Bring broth to a brisk simmer, but not a full boil, and add clams. Cook for 2 minutes. Add mussels and fish. Cook for 2 more minutes. Add shrimp. Cook for 2 more minutes. If some ingredients are cooked before the rest, remove them. When clams and mussels begin to open, add scallops, cook for 1 minute and pour mixture over large sourdough bread cubes.

Loaded Paella

Paella is a great dish to serve while entertaining. While there are many ingredients that make up the dish, the actual act of preparing it is relatively easy and can be done on your stove in the kitchen, or even on a barbecue grill in the back yard. Perfect for cool winter nights.

Serves 8 to 10

Ingredients:

- 1 tablespoon Spanish paprika
- 2 teaspoons dried oregano
- Salt and pepper to taste
- ½ bunch of cilantro, chopped coarsely
- 3 pounds chicken thighs and breasts, bone-on with skin
- 1 pound Chorizo sausage, in the casing, thickly sliced
- 2 lobster tails, cut into large chunks
- 12-14 fresh clams, scrubbed and purged in salted water
- 12-20 fresh mussels, scrubbed and purged in salted water
- 2 pounds of shrimp, peeled and deveined
- 1 Spanish onion, diced
- 6 cloves of garlic, crushed
- 4 tomatoes, diced
- 1 10-ounce package of frozen green peas, defrosted
- 2-4 tablespoons Tabasco sauce,
    - add more or less depending upon your tolerance for heat
- 1 pinch saffron threads, approximately ¼ gram
- up to 4 cups uncooked, short grained white rice *(I recommend California Pearl rice.)* Use 1 cup of rice for every 2 ¼ cups of water added to the pot)
- up to 9 cups of water

Preparation:

For this dish, you need to invest in a paella pan, called a paellera, a round "deep dish" frying pan with handles on two sides, and a tight-fitting lid.

Mix together the paprika, oregano, salt and pepper, and coat chicken breasts and thighs with spice mixture. Heat a paella pan over medium-high heat, and add sliced chorizo. Once chorizo has browned, remove chorizo from pan and set aside. Add the chicken and garlic to the pan and stir until nicely browned. Move the browned meat to the sides of the pan, and add the tomato and onion. Sautéing until onions are soft and translucent.

Since paella pans come in different sizes, add up to 9 cups of water to your pan, measuring the water as you put it in the pan. Bring mixture to a boil, then reduce heat and simmer for 45 minutes to 1 hour, or until chicken starts to fall off the bone.

Season with a generous amount of salt, Tabasco, and a pinch of saffron. Stir in 1 cup of rice for every 2 ¼ cups of water that you originally added to the paellera. Bring rice to a boil, stir, and place clams, mussels, and lobster chunks in pan. Cover, reduce heat to low, and simmer until most all of the liquid has been absorbed, about 14 minutes. (Clams and mussels should be just beginning to open.) Add shrimp and cooked chorizo chunks to mixture. Stir quickly, and cover. Cook for approximately 10 more minutes until all of the juice has been incorporated into the rice.

Add defrosted green peas to paella. Stir quickly. Leaving uncovered, turn heat up to high for 3-5 minutes, or until you can smell the rice toast at the bottom of the pan, called socarrat. Remove from heat. Garnish with chopped cilantro. Enjoy!

Seared Scallops with White Beans and Pancetta

When cooked properly, scallops are amazing. For this recipe, I recommend purchasing dry (not brined), sea scallops that are sized 10 to a pound or a little larger. Fresh scallops should be translucent and glistening without a milky grey tinge, and should have a clean, salty aroma. If you're not going to cook the scallops immediately, remove the scallops from their packaging and store them in the refrigerator in a sealed container. If fresh, the scallops should last for at least 2 days.

Makes 4 servings

Ingredients:

- 1 ½ pounds of jumbo scallops
- 1 14-ounce can of white beans, rinsed
- ¼ pound pancetta, chopped
- 1 clove of garlic, chopped
- ½ red onion, minced
- 6 cups of baby spinach, washed
- 4 tablespoons vegetable oil
- 4 tablespoons butter
- 2 tablespoons sugar
- salt and pepper to taste

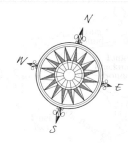

Preparation:

Place white beans and 2 cups of water in a small sauce pot on the stove over medium heat. Add salt, pepper, and half of the diced pancetta. Cook over medium heat for 10-15 minutes, reduce heat, cover, and simmer. Add more water to the beans if necessary. Dry the scallops off with a paper towel, and press the scallops into the sugar laced with salt and pepper. Set scallops aside until ready to cook. In a medium sauté pan, place the oil and remaining pancetta on the stove over medium high heat. Cook for 10 to 12 minutes, until the pancetta is crispy. Add the onions and garlic to the pan and sauté for 2 to 3 minutes until the onion is soft and translucent. Pour off approximately 2/3 of the oil from the sauté pan and set aside (to sear the scallops in).

Add the spinach to the sauté pan and stir quickly, remove from heat, cover and set aside. Place reserved oil in another sauté pan and place on stove over medium high heat. Allow the oil to get very hot. If oil begins to smoke, reduce heat. Place scallops in hot sauté pan and sear scallops on both sides for 2 to 3 minutes per side. Ideally, the center of the scallop should be just a little raw (medium) when removed from the sauté pan. Place spinach and onion mixture on plates. Then, using a slotted spoon, place white beans on plates. Top spinach and white beans with seared scallops and serve.

Note: For nicely seared scallops, do not move scallops while searing. Turn scallops only once for optimal caramelization.

Florida Orange Glazed Chicken with Cilantro

This is one of the dishes that I created for the progressive dinner during Key Largo Conch Republic Days. Chicken is one of the hardest meats to cook, as it is often dry and rubbery, or juicy and undercooked. The secret to chicken is the brine. The chicken is crisp, juicy and flavorful. Try it, and let me know. Enjoy!

Makes 4 servings

Ingredients:

- 4 skin-on chicken breasts, preferably de-boned
- 4 Key limes, sliced
- 1 Florida orange, sliced
- ½ gallon warm water
- 1/3 cup Kosher salt
- 1/3 cup extra virgin olive oil
- 3-4 tablespoons butter
- fresh cracked black pepper to taste
- ½ bunch cilantro, chopped
- 4 green onions, diced

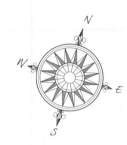

Preparation:

Place warm water and Kosher salt into a container large enough to hold chicken breasts and brine mixture. Allow water to come to room temperature, and add chicken breasts, orange and Key lime slices. Cover and place in the refrigerator, at least 8 hours before cooking (you can either do this the morning of, or the night before). Remove chicken breasts from brine and dry breasts with a kitchen towel. Make sure that the skin is stretched across the breasts, and season breasts with cracked black pepper to taste. Pre-heat oven to 350° F.

Place a large heavy sauté pan on the stove over medium-high heat. Add olive oil to pan and allow oil to get very hot. Add chicken breasts, skin side down to sauté pan. When the skin has a nice golden color, turn the chicken breast over. Add the butter to the sauté pan, and spoon butter-oil mixture over chicken breasts for 2-3 minutes. Place sauté pan in the oven and continue to cook for 8 minutes or until the breast meat at the thickest part of the breasts is 165° F. Remove from oven. Brush breasts with orange glaze, sprinkle with chopped cilantro, green onions, and serve with black beans, rice, and diced tomatoes.

Florida Orange Glaze

Ingredients:

- ¾ cup orange marmalade
- 2 tablespoons soy sauce
- 2 Florida oranges, juiced (save rind for zest)
- 1 tablespoon orange zest

Preparation:

Place a small sauce pan on the stove over medium heat. Add marmalade, soy sauce, fresh orange juice, and orange zest into sauce pan. Stirring occasionally, cook until mixture begins to boil. Reduce heat to low, and simmer for approximately 10 minutes. Remove from heat, and strain glaze through a strainer to create a smooth glaze (optional).

Chicken & Yellow Rice

Your guests or family will love this homemade chicken and yellow rice. Even the yellow rice is made from scratch with this recipe. It is sure to quickly become a family favorite.

Makes 4-6 Servings

Ingredients:

- 2 cups short grained white or pear rice
- 1 whole chicken, approximately 2 ½ pounds
- 2 tablespoons chopped garlic in oil
- 8 cups water
- 1 medium Spanish onion, chopped
- 1 red bell pepper, chopped
- 1 green bell pepper, chopped
- 1 tablespoon olive oil
- 1 pinch saffron
- 1 small bag frozen peas, approximately 8 ounces
- salt and pepper to taste

Preparation:

Place chicken, water, garlic, salt and pepper into a large pot and place on stove over high heat. While chicken is cooking, make sofrito by placing chopped onion, peppers, and olive oil into a sauté pan, and sauté over medium heat until onions are translucent. Remove from heat and set sofrito aside. Boil chicken until it is falling off of the bone, then remove chicken from broth and allow chicken pieces to cool. Place rice, saffron, and sofrito into the chicken broth over high heat. Stirring occasionally, bring mixture to a boil for 2 minutes. Reduce heat to low and cover tightly for 12 minutes. Remove cover, add peas and cooked chicken. Stir well, recover and cook for approximately 3 minutes, or until all liquid has been incorporated into the rice, and the rice is soft. Remove from heat. Serve and enjoy!

Optional: While rice is cooking, you may want to remove the chicken meat from the bones. Discard the skin and bones, and just add the chicken meat to the rice.

Key West Pink Shrimp au Gratin

Great for cool winter nights, this dish is warm and savory, made with the shrimp that made the Key West shrimping industry famous. Of course, you can substitute regular shrimp for this dish, or substitute lobster chunks…amazing!

- 1 ½ pounds of peeled and deveined Key West pink shrimp, tails removed
- 1 tablespoon vegetable oil
- 4 tablespoons butter
- 1-2 teaspoons Sundowners' Black Caesar's Blackening Spice (recipe page 73)
- ½ teaspoon Kosher salt
- ½ teaspoon white pepper
- 3 cloves of garlic, chopped
- 2 ½ tablespoons all-purpose flour
- 2 Key limes, juiced
- 1 ¼ cups milk
- ⅔ cup heavy cream
- 1 ½ cups shredded Monterey jack cheese
- 2 scallions, chopped
- 2 tablespoons onion, minced
- 1 ½ cup panko bread crumbs

Preparation:

Preheat oven to 400° F. Lightly grease eight 6-8 ounce ramekins or one small-to-medium Pyrex bowl. Dust shrimp with blackening spice and a pinch of salt and white pepper (holding back about ½ of the salt and pepper for the final dish). In a large skillet, large enough to hold all of the shrimp, heat the vegetable oil and 1 tablespoon of the butter on high heat. Once oil is hot, toss shrimp into pan and cook for approximately 1 minute per side. Shrimp should still be medium rare when removed from pan. Divide shrimp evenly among ramekins or place in bottom of Pyrex bowl. In a small sauce pan over medium heat, melt the remaining butter. Add the onions and garlic and cook until onions are translucent. Add the flour to the butter mixture and stir quickly to incorporate the flour, being careful not to let the flour brown. Add the milk and cream to the mixture slowly and continue stirring. Cook for 5-6 minutes, or until the flour taste is gone from your cream mixture. Add Key lime juice, 1 cup shredded cheese, scallions, and salt and pepper to taste. Remove from heat and spoon over shrimp. In a small bowl mix remaining cheese and bread crumbs. Top each ramekin or Pyrex dish with the bread crumb mixture. Place dish(es) on a large baking sheet and bake for 15 to 20 minutes, until golden brown and bubbly. Enjoy!

Churasco Steak with Chimichurri Sauce

The Hispanic influences in South Florida, and the freshness of the ingredients, make this recipe for beef lovers a favorite in the Keys. Chimichurri is a garlicky sauce from Argentina that is great when spooned over grilled, marinated flank steak or chicken. For the skirt steak, we are using a marinade recipe that has more in common with Italian cooking than with Spanish food, but the sweetness of the marinade compliments the bitterness of the chimichurri nicely.

Makes 4 servings

Ingredients:

2 ½ pounds trimmed skirt steak (skirt steak is the best, but you can use this recipe on flank, rib eye, or New York Strips as well)
½ cup vegetable oil
½ cup olive oil
3 tablespoons garlic, chopped
3 tablespoons Coleman's dry mustard
½ cup brown sugar
2 teaspoons salt
½ teaspoon ground pepper

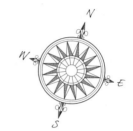

Preparation:

Place all ingredients, except for steak, in a large mixing bowl and mix well. Cut skirt steaks into approximately 8 to 10-inch pieces. Pour marinade into a 1-gallon Ziplock bag, and add skirt steak pieces. Seal bag and place in refrigerator for at least 3 hours. Shake bag occasionally to ensure that the steaks are well coated with marinade. Preheat barbecue grill and place steaks. Grill steaks to desired temperature. Serve steaks with Chimichurri Sauce on the side.

Chimichurri Sauce

Ingredients:

1 bunch Italian parsley, chopped
1 bunch cilantro, chopped
½ cup olive oil
1 cup balsamic vinegar
2 garlic cloves, chopped
¾ teaspoon dried crushed red pepper
½ teaspoon salt

Preparation:

For this recipe, I prefer to coarsely chop all vegetables. Fresh garlic, instead of garlic in oil, makes a huge difference in this dish. Place all ingredients into a small mixing bowl, and mix well. Use a fork or slotted spoon to remove the vegetables from the oil when you are ready to serve.

Tamarind-Rubbed Pork Tenderloin

Pork tenderloin, like chicken breast, is another one of those items that I like to brine before cooking. The brine helps to ensure that the pork is both tender and juicy when it is finished. This recipe, created for a gourmet meal at Señor Frijoles, combines the sweetness of the tamarind with a little spice, which goes nicely with the pork.

Makes 4 servings

Ingredients:

- 1 (2 pound) pork tenderloin
- 1 cup Kosher salt
- 2 tablespoons olive oil

Procedure:

Place pork tenderloin into a bowl and cover with water. Add salt and allow pork to brine for at least 8 hours and up to 2 days. Remove pork from brine, and rinse with fresh water.

Preheat oven to 400° F. Heat olive oil in a large sauté pan over high heat (best if you have a cast iron skillet). Sear the pork on all sides until golden brown. Remove pork from the skillet and allow it to cool for just a few minutes. Rub pork loin with tamarind rub and place in oven to finish cooking for 8 to 10 minutes or until tenderloin reaches and internal temperature of 145° F. Remove tenderloin from oven and allow to rest for 10 minutes, slicing on a bias. Serve and enjoy!

TAMARIND RUB

Ingredients:

- 2 tablespoons tamarind paste
- 3 tablespoons brown sugar
- 4 cloves garlic, chopped
- 2 tablespoons olive oil
- 1 tablespoon chili powder
- 1 teaspoon Cayenne pepper

Procedure:

Mix all ingredients together in a bowl.

Palomilla Steak

This dish explores a traditional Cuban delicacy: Palomilla Steak, or Bistec de Palomilla. While budget conscious, this dish is both flavorful and tender. Serve with black beans and rice, or crispy homefries, and extra Key limes.

Makes 4 servings

Ingredients:

- 4 sirloin steaks, 10-12-ounces each, cut thin (½ inch or less)
- 12-14 Key limes, juice 10-12 Key limes (approximately 1 cup),
    reserve 2 Key limes and cut into wedges for the steaks,
    reserve 1 tablespoon of Key lime juice for Key lime butter
- 1 cup olive oil
- 8 tablespoons vegetable oil (can substitute olive oil,
    but vegetable oil has a lighter flavor)
- 1 teaspoon oregano
- 1 large head of garlic, peeled, and chopped
- salt and pepper to taste
- 2 large onions, peeled and sliced into rings
- 2 ounces dry white wine
- 1 bunch of cilantro, chopped
- 4 tablespoons butter

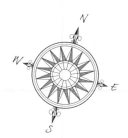

Preparation:

Pat steaks dry and wrap individually in Saran wrap. Using the flat side of a butcher's mallet, pound the steaks until tenderized and no more than ¼ inch thick. Try not to pound "holes" into the steaks. Remove from Saran wrap, and salt and pepper both sides. Place lime juice (remember to hold back 1 tablespoon of Key lime juice for Key lime butter), olive oil, oregano, chopped garlic, and 1 tablespoon of chopped cilantro into a large Ziplock bag or into a shallow pan. Place steaks into the Ziplock or pan and place into refrigerator.

Turning steaks occasionally, allow steaks to marinate for at least two hours (steaks can be left in marinade for up to 12 hours). Remove steaks from marinade and allow steaks to come to room temperature before cooking. Place a large sauté pan on the stove over medium-high heat, and add 2 tablespoons of vegetable oil, sliced onion rings, and salt and pepper. Remove onions from heat, once onions begin to become translucent. Onions should be soft, but still firm enough to hold their shape. While onions are cooking, place a cast iron skillet on the stove over high heat, and heat pan until very hot. Add 2-4 tablespoons of vegetable oil to cast iron skillet.

Remove room-temperature steaks from marinade, and shake off excess marinade, pat dry if necessary. Place steaks in cast iron skillet and cook in batches for approximately 2 minutes per side. If your skillet is hot enough, the steaks will have brown "crispy" patches on both sides of the steaks. Remove steaks from skillet and place on a large serving platter. Keep warm while you finish the rest of the steaks.

Allow your skillet to get back to temperature, before you begin the second batch of steaks. When all steaks are finished cooking, add butter and wine to cast iron skillet. Add the remaining tablespoon of Key lime juice, and cook until butter mixture begins to bubble. Top steaks with onions and Key lime butter. Finish off with a generous amount of cilantro, and serve with Key lime wedges on the side.

contributed photo

Mangrove Honey & Chipotle Glazed Rib Eye

This amazing dish is a favorite among beef lovers at Marker 88. The smokiness of the chipotle and the sweetness of the honey provide a perfect balance.

Makes 4 servings

Ingredients:

4 prime grade, rib-eye steaks, 14-to-16-ounces each, or
    22-24 ounce bone-in "cowboy" rib eye steaks for more flavor
½ cup mangrove honey, or other honey (there's a big difference
    in the flavor of honey, so make sure you buy one that you really like)
1 tablespoon, chipotle puree
1 tablespoon Zatarain's Creole Mustard
¼ cup of vegetable oil
salt and pepper to taste

Preparation:

Place honey, chipotle puree, dry mustard, and vegetable oil into a bowl, and whisk until well blended. Salt and pepper rib eye steaks and place on a hot barbecue grill over high heat. Cook steaks to temperature, brushing steaks with glaze while cooking. Remove from grill, and serve.

Ballyhoo's Coconut Milk Marinated Chicken

The next time you have a barbecue, try this great dish from Ballyhoo's restaurant. The coconut milk ads a little sweetness to the chicken and makes the chicken wonderfully moist. For those of you who do not like the flavor of coconut, have no fear, because the cooking process removes all of the coconut flavor from the finished dish. While this recipe calls for chicken breasts cut into strips, this marinade works well with any type of chicken: wings, whole roasted, bone-in thighs…I think you get the idea.

Makes 4 servings

Ingredients:

   2 pounds of boneless, skinless chicken breasts
   12 ounces unsweetened coconut milk
   1 cup Italian dressing (bottled or homemade, the choice is yours)

Preparation:

Place chicken breasts into a bowl and cover with coconut milk and Italian dressing. Stir well so that the chicken breasts are covered with the marinade. Cover and place into refrigerator. Allow chicken to marinate for at least 2 hours. Grill on a pre-heated barbecue grill over medium high heat until chicken is white throughout and at least 165° F. Allow grilled chicken to "rest" for approximately 10 minutes after cooking.

Picadillo with Sweet Corn Polenta Mashed Potatoes "Cuban Style Shepherd's Pie"

This recipe is twist on picadillo and shepherd's pie, and is a great dish on a cool winter night in the Florida Keys. Feel free to make just the picadillo recipe below and serve it over rice, or go for the gusto and make the entire dish.

Makes 4 servings

PICADILLO

Ingredients:

- 2 pounds lean ground beef
- 1 teaspoon cumin
- 2 teaspoons whole oregano
- 2 teaspoons chili powder
- 4 tablespoons Spanish olive oil
- 10-12 cloves fresh garlic, smashed and chopped
- 1 medium Spanish onion, diced
- 1 large green pepper, diced with seeds removed
- 2 cups beef stock
- 4 bay leaves
- 1 6 ounce can tomato sauce
- 2 -6 ounce jars of pimento-stuffed Spanish olives, slice olives into thirds
- ½ bunch cilantro, chopped
- salt and pepper to taste

(Traditional picadillo also contains potatoes (2 peeled and diced) added to the dish with the meat, however we have left this out of our picadillo as we are topping the picadillo with Sweet Corn Polenta Mashed Potatoes)

Preparation:

In a large frying pan, sauté onions, garlic, and chopped bell peppers to create the "sofrito" for the dish. Sauté until onions are translucent. Add the ground beef, beef stock, and tomato sauce (and potatoes if making just picadillo). Sauté on high for approximately 15 minutes, stirring frequently until beef is well browned. Reduce heat to simmer and add cumin, whole oregano, chili powder, and bay leaves. Simmer for 15-20 minutes as the liquids in the pan continue to reduce. Add the sliced olives, cilantro, and salt and pepper to taste. Simmer for 10-15 minutes, or until the picadillo is decently dry.

Note: some prefer their picadillo a little wet, while others prefer it very dry, the choice is yours on when to remove the picadillo from the stove.

Sweet Corn Polenta Mashed Potatoes

Ingredients:

4 medium potatoes, peeled, salted and boiled
3 cups of fresh or frozen, cut off the cob, corn kernels
2 cups of water
2 teaspoons salt
½ teaspoon pepper
2-3 tablespoons honey
2 cups corn grits (or polenta)
6-8 tablespoons butter
1 cup heavy cream

Preparation:

Prepare the polenta by bringing water and salt to a boil, and slowly adding polenta. Reduce heat to a simmer, and stir polenta frequently. Simmer for approximately 15 minutes, then slowly add ½ of the heavy cream, pepper, butter, honey, and corn. Using a fork or potato masher, mash cooked potatoes and add to polenta mixture. These potatoes should be the consistency of "soft" mashed potatoes. If necessary, slowly add more heavy cream, salt or pepper. Place picadillo into a Pyrex casserole dish. Top with polenta mashed potatoes, and place into a preheated oven at 350° F. Bake for 15-20 minutes, or until potatoes are nicely browned. Remove from oven, cool for a few minutes

Marinated Key Lime Turkey

What makes this turkey recipe unique is the addition of homemade, preserved Key limes. The limes, and garlic butter, add a delicious, surprising zip to your holiday turkey.

PRESERVED KEY LIMES (make 2 weeks in advance)

Ingredients:

1-2 bags of fresh Key limes
Kosher salt
paprika
1 large pickling or preserve jar

Preparation:

Wash Key limes well, and cut in half. Begin to layer lime halves into a clean, large pickling or preserve jar and top each layer with Kosher salt (to coat) and a dash of paprika. Continue to layering process until all limes have been used, or until the jar is full (you can pack the limes in here as it helps them to begin to release their juice). Cover the limes with fresh Key lime juice, leaving a small amount of air in the preserve jar. Shake jar at least once a day for at least 2 weeks, or until the skin of the limes have softened. When ready to use, quickly rinse limes. Use skins and/or pulp in butters, sauces, soups, atop fish, or as we are here, with turkey or chicken.

KEY LIME TURKEY BRINE

Ingredients:

1 gallon of water
1 cup Kosher salt
½ cup of preserved lime juice (from recipe above)
½ cup apple cider vinegar
3 tablespoons brown sugar
1 tablespoon pickling spice
1 teaspoon ground all spice
1 teaspoon garlic powder
1 teaspoon tarragon
1 teaspoon sage (fresh or dry)
6-8 preserved Key lime halves

Preparation:

Place water, salt and brown sugar into a large pot, and bring to a boil, stirring to incorporate the salt and the sugar. Remove from the stove and allow water to cool. Add vinegar, preserved lime juice, lime halves, and spices. Place your turkey in brine and brine under refrigeration for 10 – 12 hours, or brine for 1 hour per pound of turkey.

TURKEY

Ingredients:

1 10 to 12-pound turkey (or larger if you prefer)
1 small head of garlic (cleaned, and roasted until soft)
1 stick of butter, softened to room temperature
4-5 sprigs of fresh sage
the leafy tops of 4-5 celery stalks
1 cup of preserved Key lime juice
10-12 preserved Key lime halves
Salt and pepper to taste

Preparation:

Prepare garlic butter, by mixing mashed roasted garlic cloves, butter, and salt and pepper to taste. Pre-heat oven to 325° F. Rinse and pat turkey dry both inside and out, removing neck and turkey innards. Salt and pepper turkey cavity, and spoon 2-3 tablespoons of garlic butter inside cavity. Place celery leaves, sage, and 4-5 preserved Key lime halves inside cavity. Starting at the neck end of the turkey, carefully pull back the skin of the turkey and spoon garlic butter over the breast, thighs, and drumsticks, on both sides.

Place a few preserved Key limes on top of the garlic butter, and replace skin (the skin will help to hold the limes in place). Tie legs together and tuck in wings. Place turkey on a baking rack, spread remaining butter on the outside of the turkey, and place any remaining preserved Key limes on top of the turkey. Pour 1 cup of preserved Key lime juice into the roasting pan. Cover turkey and bake for 15-20 minutes per pound, or until a thermometer inserted into the thickest part of the turkey breast reads 150° F.

Remove cover, baste turkey with drippings and return turkey to oven to brown for at least another ½ hour, or until a thermometer inserted into the thickest part of the breast reads 165° to 170° F. Remove turkey from oven, and cover with tented foil for 30 minutes. Carve and serve!

DESSERTS

Key Lime Sweets Fruits & Confections

Refreshing Florida Keys Desserts

Sundowners' World-Famous Key Lime Pie

Key lime pie is famous throughout the world, and in fact is one of the most popular desserts on menus throughout the United States. As a kid, growing up in the Keys, you would think that we had Key lime pie at every meal, but this was not the case. We reserved it for special occasions. (We had Key lime cake with every meal!). One of the unique things about original Key lime pie recipes was that the pies were never baked. The lime juice curdles the sweetened condensed milk and helps to "set" the pie. Today, however, we bake all of the pies.

Makes 1 pie

Ingredients:

    4 egg yolks
    14 ounces sweetened condensed milk
    ½ cup + 4 tablespoons fresh Key lime juice (approximately 20 Key limes)
    11 graham crackers (crushed fine)
    3 tablespoons Demura sugar
    5 tablespoons high quality, unsalted butter, softened or melted

Preparation:

To crush the graham crackers, use a blender or food processor, and process until graham crackers are crushed fine. Place crushed graham crackers on a baking pan and toast in a 350° F oven until they begin to brown, approximately 3 to 4 minutes. Remove graham crackers from the oven. Place graham crackers into a mixing bowl and mix in Demura sugar with a fork until well blended. In another bowl, pour graham cracker mixture over softened butter, while graham crackers are still warm, and continue to mix with a fork until all of the butter has been incorporated into the crust mixture. Press graham cracker crust into a 9-inch pie pan, ensuring that the crust is an even depth throughout the pie pan (and up the sides if you prefer). Set pie crust aside.

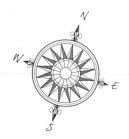

In a large mixing bowl, mix sweetened condensed milk with egg yolks. Add ½ cup of fresh Key lime juice to milk mixture and mix well. Remember to save at least 4 tablespoons of fresh Key Lime juice for "topping the pie." Set Key lime pie mixture aside, and allow the mixture to thicken.

Place your homemade crust into a 350° F oven for approximately 10-15 minutes until crust is lightly brown. This double toasting of the graham crackers helps to enhance the consistency of your crust and brings out the flavor of the graham crackers. Allow crust to cool to room temperature before adding Key lime filling. Pour the filling into the crust and spread evenly. Bake at 350° F for 15 minutes or until the center of the pie is "set" but still jiggles when shaken.

Remove Key lime pie from oven and allow pie to cool to room temperature before refrigerating. Refrigerate for 2-3 hours before serving. For best results, top Key lime pie with homemade meringue or homemade Key lime whipped cream. Just before serving, drizzle Key lime pie slices with remaining Key lime juice.

144 | Recipes & Tall Tales from Legendary Restaurants of the Florida Keys

Key Lime Fudge

Every time we serve this fudge to our guests, they love it. The recipe does not require a candy thermometer like most fudge recipes call for. Rich, creamy, with just a hint of Key lime. Perfect for the holidays, or any time that you want just a taste of the Florida Keys. This recipe is also great with fresh, Florida orange juice, and oranges in place of the Key limes.

Ingredients:

- 14 ounces sweetened condensed milk
- 2 tablespoons fresh Key lime juice (approximately 3 Key limes)
- 3 teaspoons of Key lime zest (use a microplane to keep the zest pieces small)
- 3 cups of white chocolate chips

Preparation:

Butter a casserole dish or 8x8 baking dish, and set aside. Place sweetened condensed milk and white chocolate chips into a large sauce pan and place on the stove over low heat. Stir chocolate mixture until all chocolate chips are melted and incorporated into the sweetened condensed milk. Remove from heat and stir in Key lime zest and fresh Key lime juice. Pour mixture into your prepared baking dish. Cover and chill for at least 2 hours, or until Key lime fudge is "set" and hard. Remove from the refrigerator and enjoy!

Mango Pie

In Georgia, they have peach pies, and in the rest of the USA they have apple pies. In South Florida, we grow mangos, so we have mango pies. Made just like a peach or apple pie, they are amazing!

CRUST *(of course you could cheat and purchase frozen premade crust)*

Ingredients:

- 2 ½ cups all-purpose flour, plus a little flour for rolling
- 3 tablespoons sugar
- 1 teaspoon salt
- 1 teaspoon grated lemon zest
- 1 cup unsalted butter, cut into small pieces, and kept cold
- ½ cup ice cold water

Prepare crust by mixing flour, sugar, salt and lemon zest. Cut butter into flour to form coarse crumbs. Add ice water, a few tablespoons at a time and continue mixing dough until mixture starts to come together. Form dough into a large ball and divide into two parts. Press dough into disks and wrap each disk in plastic wrap. Refrigerate dough for 30 minutes before rolling out one of the dough disks into the bottom pie shell. Preheat oven to 350° F. Place rolled out dough into a 9 inch deep-dish pie pan. Trim edges. Place another pie pan (I use glass so I can see through it) on top of crust to weight down crust and bake until crust is a light golden brown. Remove pie weight and sprinkle crust with flour and bake 5 minutes longer. Fill with mango pie filling below. Roll out the remaining dough and fit over pie. Crimp edges and brush the top of the pie crust with egg wash. Cut vent holes into top of pie and bake for 45 to 50 minutes, or until crust is golden brown and filling is bubbly. Serve with vanilla ice cream. Enjoy!

MANGO FILLING

- 5 large ripe Kent mangos, peeled and cut into ¾ inch slices
- ½ cup sugar
- 2 teaspoons cinnamon
- 2 tablespoons flour
- 1 tablespoon almond extract
- 2 Key limes, juiced (and the zest from 1 key lime)

Place all ingredients into a medium-sized mixing bowl and toss well. Mixture should be moist but not wet.

EGG WASH

- 1 egg
- 3 tablespoons of water

Crack egg into a small bowl. Add water and mix well. Use a brush to egg wash the top of your pie crust.

Key Lime Raspberry Squares

This one is an old favorite from Señor Frijoles' kitchen.

Ingredients:

1/2 lb. unsalted butter, softened
1/2 cup confectioners sugar (plus a little for garnish)
2-1/3 cups all-purpose flour
3 pints raspberries
4 eggs plus 1 egg yolk
3 cups granulated sugar
1/3 cup Key lime juice
1 teaspoon baking powder

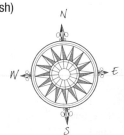

Preparation:

Place raspberries and 1 cup of sugar into a pan and place on stove. Cook over medium-low heat stirring occasionally, until all sugar has been incorporated into mixture, and raspberries are soft. Mixture should be hot, but should not boil. Remove from stove, allow to cool, and then puree in a blender or food processor. Cream butter and confectioners sugar until light and fluffy. Add 2 cups flour and stir until a soft dough forms. Pat into a prepared 9x13 baking pan and bake 15 min., at 350° F until firm but not brown. Cool in pan on rack. Spread with raspberry compote, leaving a 1/4 inch border.

Whisk eggs and yolk until foamy. Whisk in granulated sugar, Key lime juice, remaining flour and baking powder. Pour egg mixture over compote and bake 30-35 minutes, until topping is set and lightly browned. Sprinkle top with confectioners sugar, cool, and cut into bars.

Profiteroles

The dough used to make this recipe is called "pâte à choux," and it is the basic dough recipe behind cream puffs and éclairs. While this is a decently technical recipe to prepare, it is actually quite easy and the end result is pretty amazing. Fill your profiteroles with Key lime cream, as described below, or try orange chocolate mousse or even pastry cream.

Ingredients:

1 cup water
½ cup (1 stick) unsalted butter
1 teaspoon sugar
pinch salt
1 cup sifted all-purpose flour
1 teaspoon baking powder
3 large eggs

Preparation:

Place a heavy-bottomed saucepan on the stove over medium-high heat. Add water, butter, salt and sugar and bring to a gentle boil, stirring to melt the butter completely. Add the flour and baking soda and continue to stir until all the flour has been incorporated in the mixture and the dough begins to pull away from the sides of the pot. Do not let the mixture burn. Remove from heat and scrape the dough into a mixing bowl and mix using a hand-held or standing mixer on medium heat, to cool the dough. Add the eggs, slowly, scraping the sides of the bowl periodically until all eggs have been incorporated into the dough. The dough should be glossy and thick.

Line 2 baking sheets with parchment paper, and preheat the oven to 400° F.

Form 24 golf-ball-size mounds of dough on the baking sheets, 2 inches apart using a small scoop or spoon to form pastry balls. leaving the balls as tall as possible. Place the pans in the oven and bake for 10 minutes. Reduce the heat to 350° F and continue to cook for 25 more minutes. Do not open the oven door until the puffs are golden brown, well-risen, and firm to the touch, as you do not want the pastry to fall during the cooking process.

Allow the shells to cool before filling. Cut profiteroles in half and fill with Key Lime Cream. Replace top and stack on a plate. Place profiteroles into freezer and allow the cream to set for at least 30 minutes before serving. Remove profiteroles from freezer and top with warm ganache. Serve immediately.

contributed photo

KEY LIME CREAM

Ingredients:

12 ounces non-dairy whipped topping (cool whip)
4 ounces fresh key lime juice (add more or less depending on your taste)
1 can sweetened condensed milk

Preparation:

Mix sweetened condensed milk and key lime juice together. Gently fold in whipped topping.

CHOCOLATE GANACHE

(prepare just before serving profiteroles)

Ingredients:

4 ounces bittersweet chocolate
2 teaspoons brandy or Grand Marnier
½ cup heavy whipping cream
1 tablespoon unsalted butter

Preparation:

Place cream and butter into a small sauce pan and heat over medium heat. Bring just to a boil and then immediately remove from heat. Place chocolate pieces into a stainless steel bowl and pour hot cream mixture over chocolate. Allow to stand for a few minutes to soften chocolate, then stir with a whisk until ganache is smooth and all chocolate has been incorporated.

Desserts

Key Lime Baked Alaska

For over 25 years, Marker 88 has been serving this Florida Keys version of Baked Alaska. Sweet and tart, it's a suprise your family and guests will enjoy.

Makes 10-12 Servings

Unless you have a blast freezer, this recipe takes 3 days to make!

Ingredients:

- 4 egg yolks
- 1 14-ounce can sweetened condensed milk
- 3/4 cup Key lime juice
- 1/2 gallon "brick" of vanilla ice cream

FROSTING

- 4 egg whites
- 1/2 teaspoon cream of tartar
- 1/2 cup sugar

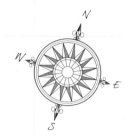

Preparation:

Cut the ice cream into two 1-inch thick sheets and place each sheet of ice cream into a separate 12x5 bread pan. Allow ice cream to melt until it is the consistency of uncooked cake mix. Add 1/4 cup of fresh Key Lime juice to one of the pans (pan a) and place both bread pans into the freezer to freeze overnight. Prepare the Key lime filling by beating egg yolks, then folding in the sweetened condensed milk and 1/2 cup of fresh Key lime juice. Spread this filling over the ice cream in the bread pan that does not have the Key lime juice (pan b). Freeze overnight. Take both pans out of freezer and remove the Key lime ice cream from "pan a" and place on top of the ice cream with the Key lime pie filling (pan b).

Place "pan b" back into the freezer for at least 1 hour. Preheat oven to 500° F. Prepare frosting by beating egg whites with the cream of tartar until they are very stiff. Slowly add the sugar, and continue to beat until egg whites are stiff enough to form peaks. Take "pan b" out of the freezer and turn upside down onto a cool oven-proof platter. Frost Key lime ice cream mold with merengue (approximately 1/2 inch thick). Place Baked Alaska platter on a wood bread or pizza board, to help insulate the ice cream during the baking process. Place in oven and bake for up to 5 minutes, watching carefully. Remove as soon as the meringue begins to brown. Squeeze fresh Key limes over dessert and serve immediately.

Florida Strawberry & Peach "Melba"

This is a recipe I prepared for one of the famous families of Key Largo. It was her birthday after all, and I thought of surprising her with one of her favorite desserts, Peach Melba, but with a Florida twist.

Makes 4 Servings

Ingredients:

- 3 cups water
- 1 cup local honey
- 8 cloves
- 2 cups sugar
- 1 Costa Rica vanilla bean, split
- 3 Key limes, juiced
- 6-8 ripe peaches, quartered with the pits removed
- 3 cups Florida strawberries
- 1 gallon vanilla bean ice cream

Preparation:

Place the water, ½ cup honey, sugar, 3 tablespoons Key lime juice, cloves, and split vanilla bean into a large sauté pan and heat gently to dissolve the sugar. Bring the syrup to a boil, and let it boil for 5 minutes. Turn heat down to simmer. Place peach quarters in the syrup to simmer for 2 to 3 minutes on each side depending on the ripeness of the fruit, until the peaches are warm throughout and soft. Once the peaches are poached, peel off their skins and let them cool. Place the strawberries, ½ cup honey, and 1 tablespoon of Key lime juice in a blender, and blend until smooth. Place peach quarters on a refrigerated plate alongside a scoop of ice cream. Spoon the strawberry sauce generously, over each.

Strawberry Bruschetta on Raisin Bread Toast

Ingredients:

- 1 cup strawberries, hulled and diced
- 1 tablespoon Demura sugar
- 1 loaf of raisin bread cut into finger sandwich sized slices, well toasted
- ¼ cup mint leaves, cut into ribbons
- 4 ounces mascarpone cheese
- 1 tablespoon mangrove honey
- 1 tablespoon balsamic reduction — optional

Preparation:

Place berries and sugar into a small bowl, and toss gently. Let the berries sit for approximately 30 minutes. Spread a thin layer of mascarpone cheese on each slice of raisin bread. Drizzle with honey, and then top each slice of bread with diced strawberries. Drizzle lightly with balsamic reduction (optional) and garnish with mint leaves. Enjoy!

Chocolate Pecan Pie

Makes one pie

Ingredients:

1 unbaked 9-inch pie shell
1 cup large semisweet chocolate chips
2 ¼ cups pecans
4 eggs, at room temperature, beaten
½ cup sugar
½ cup corn syrup
½ cup brown sugar
½ teaspoon vanilla extract
pinch salt

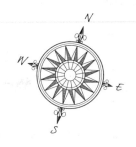

Preparation:

Preheat the oven to 375° F. In a mixing bowl, mix eggs, sugar, corn syrup, brown sugar, vanilla extract, and salt. Pour pecans and chocolate chips into a medium sized mixing bowl and mix well, then pour pecan mixture into pie shell. Pour egg mixture over the pecans slowly. Bake for approximately 50 minutes, or until the filling is "set." Remove the pie from the oven and allow to cool before slicing. Top pie with whipped cream and enjoy.

Chocolate-Orange Cuban Bread Pudding

Typically bread pudding is a heavy dessert that is all about the bread. This recipe is quite a bit different, in that it is really a pudding that is accompanied by the bread. It is best to begin this recipe at least a day ahead of time to give the bread time to soak up the cream.

Makes 6 servings

Ingredients:

- 4 cups Cuban bread, cubed
- 2 cups heavy cream
- 1 cup Half & Half
- 6 large egg yolks, at room temperature (true for all baking)
- ¾ cup sugar
- 2 ounces Grand Marnier
- 3 teaspoons fresh orange zest
- 4 ounces semisweet chocolate pieces

Preparation:

Place the orange zest and Grand Marnier into a glass to marinate. Place cream and Half & Half into a saucepan over low heat. In a mixing bowl, place egg yolks, sugar, vanilla and whisk. Add the chocolate pieces to the warm cream and stir until the chocolate has been incorporated into the cream. Add the marinated orange zest to the mixing bowl, and then slowly add the warm chocolate cream, a little at a time, to prevent the eggs from "cooking" in the warm cream. Add the bread to the bowl. Mix well, cover and refrigerate so that bread can absorb all of the pudding. Place a rack in the middle of your oven, and preheat oven to 325° F. Butter 6 six-ounce ramekins or baking dishes, and spoon mixture into the dishes. Place the ramekins in a roasting pan large enough to hold the ramekins and fill pan with warm water until the water is half way up the sides of the ramekin. Place roasting pan in the oven and bake uncovered for approximately 25 minutes, or until the custard is "set" but still wobbles a little when shaken. Remove the pan from the oven and carefully serve bread pudding while it is still warm. Top with vanilla ice cream or whipped cream. Enjoy!

Roasted Banana and Toffee Trifle

Trifles are layered desserts that are easy to make, and with a trifle bowl, or the right container, are beautiful desserts that are sure to please and impress your guests. This trifle is made with roasted bananas to give the trifle "just enough" banana flavor. The roasting process also softens the bananas, so that the banana pulp pours right out of the banana skin.

Makes 1 trifle

Ingredients:

10 ripe bananas
2 large packages of vanilla pudding mix (6 ½ cup servings)
10 ounces chopped graham crackers
4 ounces English toffee bits (or Heath candy, chopped)
6 ounces vanilla wafers
whipped cream
chocolate sundae sauce
caramel sauce
1 trifle bowl

Preparation:

Place 6 bananas, skin on, in a baking pan and place in preheated oven at 350° F. Roast bananas for approximately 25 minutes, or until bananas are very soft to the touch, and the skins are completely black. Remove bananas and set aside. While bananas are roasting, prepare vanilla pudding according to manufacturer's instructions. Break open the skin on the bananas and squeeze all of the banana pulp into the finished pudding mix. Please note that you may have to mash banana pulp a little with a fork. Once all of the banana pulp has been added to the pudding, mix well, and chill.

To prepare trifle, pour ½ of the chopped graham crackers into the trifle bowl. Line the sides of the bowl with vanilla wafers. Slice 2 bananas, and layer on top of graham crackers, then sprinkle toffee bits over the bananas. Lightly cover toffee bits with caramel and chocolate sauces. Top mixture with ½ of the banana cream. Repeat the layering process until you have created your ultimate trifle. Allow trifle to sit for approximately 20 minutes before serving (may be refrigerated). Garnish with whipped cream just before serving.

Key Lime Cake

While Key lime pie is the favorite of visitors to the Florida Keys, many of the "Conchs" and "fresh water conchs" who live in the Keys, prefer Key lime cake instead. While there are many different variations of this dessert throughout the Keys, this version is moist, flavorful, and delicious!

Makes 4 servings

Ingredients:

- 2 cups all-purpose flour
- 1 1/3 cups sugar
- 1 teaspoon baking powder
- 1/2 teaspoon baking soda
- 1 pinch of salt
- 1 small box instant Key Lime pudding mix (or lemon pudding mix)
- 5 eggs
- 1 1/3 cups vegetable oil
- 3/4 cup fresh Florida orange juice
- 1/2 teaspoon vanilla extract
- 1 teaspoon lemon extract
- 2 tablespoons fresh Key lime juice
- Zest from 2 Key limes

Key Lime Glaze
Ingredients:

- 1/3 cup fresh Key lime juice
- 1/2 cup confectioners' sugar

Preparation:

Bring eggs and orange juice to room temperature. Preheat oven to 350° F. Place dry ingredients into a mixing bowl. Add eggs, oil, orange juice, vanilla, lemon extract, Key lime zest, and 2 tablespoons fresh Key lime juice. Beat mix until well blended and then pour batter into a greased Bundt pan. Bake for approximately 30-35 minutes, or until a wooden pick, inserted into the cake comes out clean. Be careful not to over bake. Remove the cake from oven, and let the cake rest in the Bundt pan for 12-15 minutes or until the cake is just "warm."

Prepare the glaze by mixing the 1/3 cup fresh Key lime juice with 1/2 cup confectioners' sugar. Turn the cake over on a cake rack, or a broiling pan, and place a pan or plate under the rack to catch any of the glaze that runs off. Poke the top of the cake with a toothpick to help the glaze absorb. Spoon glaze over the cake and continue to reapply any drippings until all of the liquid has been absorbed. Best when served at room temperature.

BRUNCH

Breakfast & Brunch

Start your day the Florida Keys way!

Sunshine French Toast

I do not cook breakfast often, but every once in a while, when I have company come into town, I will make this Florida Keys style of French toast, just to kick their day off with a smile. The croissants and Florida orange juice, give it just the right tropical flavor.

Makes 4 servings

Ingredients:

- 4 large croissants cut in half
- 5 eggs
- 4 tablespoons concentrated orange juice
- ½ cup milk
- ½ teaspoon ground cinnamon
- 2 tablespoons of butter, for cooking
- maple syrup

Preparation:

Mix eggs, concentrated orange juice, milk, and cinnamon in a bowl. Place a large sauté pan on the stove over medium high heat, and add butter. Once butter has melted, dredge croissant halves through egg mixture, and place in sauté pan. Cook for 2-3 minutes per side. Remove from pan, once the egg batter is to your liking. Serve with real maple syrup and orange butter on the side.

ORANGE BUTTER

Ingredients:

- ½ cup of butter (1 stick), softened
- 2 tablespoons of concentrated orange juice

Preparation:

Using a fork, mix butter and concentrated orange juice until orange juice is incorporated into the butter. Place orange butter in the refrigerator until ready for use. Orange butter may be made ahead of time.

Banana Bread

This is one of the simplest recipes for banana bread I have tried, and once again, it proves that the simpler the better, as this banana bread is simply delicious.

Makes 1 loaf

Ingredients:

4 really ripe bananas (the riper the better), smashed
¾ cup sugar
⅓ cup butter, melted
1 egg
1 teaspoon vanilla
1 teaspoon baking soda
1 ½ cups all-purpose flour
pinch of salt
2 pinches of cinnamon

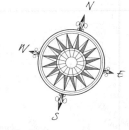

Preparation:

Preheat the oven to 350° F. In a large mixing bowl add smashed bananas, sugar, butter, vanilla, salt, cinnamon and egg. Mix well. Add baking soda and mix well. Finally, add flour and mix. Pour mixture into a buttered 4x8 inch bread pan. Bake for 1 hour, or until a toothpick inserted into the center of the bread comes out clean. Cool for at least 1 hour. Serve and enjoy!

Fresh Fruit with Florida Citrus Cream

Serve as a topping or dip with fresh fruits of your choice as a nice breakfast or lunch side. Or, as a dessert, try this cream on top of toasted pound cake with fresh strawberries and orange segments.

Ingredients:

- 2 Key limes, juiced
- 1 tablespoon fresh orange juice
- 1 teaspoon orange zest
- 1 teaspoon key lime zest
- 1 teaspoon vanilla extract
- 8 ounces cream cheese
- ½ cup whipping cream
- ¼ cup sugar

Preparation:

Place all ingredients into a medium sized mixing bowl, and using an electric mixer, beat for approximately 1 minute, or until stiff peaks form.

Lobster Benedict

Another lobster recipe. In the Keys, we have lobster everything, and lobster for breakfast is no exception. It's the price we pay for living in paradise!

Makes 4 servings

Ingredients:

- 1 tablespoon butter
- 2 (6 to 8 ounce) Florida lobster tails, boiled, shelled, and diced into chunks
- 8 slices of Canadian bacon
- 4 English muffins, split and toasted
- 8 eggs
- salt and pepper to taste

Preparation:

In a skillet melt butter over medium heat. Toss lobster meat with butter and add salt and pepper to taste. Remove lobster from skillet and keep warm. Brown Canadian bacon in the same skillet and keep warm. Poach the eggs for about 3 minutes using an egg poacher or in a pot of boiling water with 1 tablespoon of white vinegar added to the water. Do not over poach eggs as you want the yolks soft. Place English muffins open faced onto a plate and top with Canadian bacon, lobster chunks, and a soft boiled egg. Cover with Hollandaise sauce and serve!

Key Lime Hollandaise Sauce

Ingredients:

- ½ cup unsalted butter, cubed and melted
- 4 egg yolks
- 2 Key limes, juiced
- pinch of cayenne pepper
- pinch of salt

Preparation:

For this recipe, you will have to create a "double boiler" using a stainless steel bowl and a small sauce pot. Fill the sauce pot with enough water so that the water level is just below the bottom of the stainless steel bowl, when the bowl is placed on top of the sauce pot. It is important that the water not contact the bottom of your mixing bowl, as it would cook the eggs as you prepare the hollandaise. Place the sauce pot on the stove over medium-low heat. The water should be warm, but not boiling. Place eggs and lime juice into your stainless steel bowl and whisk well, until the mixture has thickened and has doubled in volume. Place stainless steel bowl on top of your sauce pot and stir, while slowly drizzling in the melted butter. Adding the butter too quickly will cause your sauce to "break" and separate. Continue whisking until all butter has been added. Sauce will thicken and double in volume. Remove from heat, whisk in cayenne pepper and salt. Taste and add more cayenne or salt if necessary.

Grits and Grunts

For breakfast many of the locals enjoy "grits and grunts." The grunts are typically caught off docks, bridges or patch reefs throughout the Keys, and locals love their light white flesh, especially when fried. Since grunts are mostly on the smaller side, their fillets too are small for some recipes, but perfect for a quick fried fish breakfast. Batter the grunts (or any white fish) using your own fish batter, or the batter from any of the fried fish recipes inside this book, and then serve the fish alongside the garlic and cheese grits casserole recipe below for an amazing Florida Keys breakfast. Eat like a local!

GARLIC CHEESE GRITS CASSEROLE

This recipe comes to me from Helen Saino of Memphis, Tennessee. Helen is the mother of Paul White, the editor of this book, and her southern cooking is almost as famous as her southern charm. Give the recipe a try and let us know what you think.

Makes 4 servings

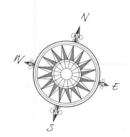

Ingredients:

1 cup old fashioned grits (not instant)
2 cups water
2 cups milk
12 ounces Monterey jack cheese, shredded
1 stick of butter
4 cloves of garlic, crushed and minced
2 eggs
¼ cup milk
Salt and pepper to taste

Preparation:

Butter a 1 ½ quart casserole dish. Pre-heat oven to 350° F. In a medium sized pot, cook grits according to instructions in water, milk and salt. When finished, grits should be pretty thick, but not dry. Remove grits from heat and add garlic, cheese, and butter and mix well. In a small bowl, place eggs, milk and salt and pepper. Beat eggs well. Add 1 tablespoon of the grits mixture to the eggs and stir well, then mix entire egg mixture into grits (this helps to keep the eggs from scrambling when added to the pot of hot grits). Pour grits mixture into casserole dish and bake for 40 to 50 minutes, or until grits are firm and are just beginning to brown on top. Remove from oven and enjoy!

Index

A

All about Conchs! 62
Amaretto Mashed Sweet Potatoes with Marshmallows 107
Andre Mueller 32
Appetizers
  Baked Oysters Barrios 56
  Charbroiled Oysters 41
  Chipotle Barbecue Sauce 52
  Cocktail Sauce 29
  Conch Egg Rolls 27
  Conch Fritters with Curry Dipping Sauce 33
  Conch Salad 30
  Cozumel Shrimp Cocktail 35
  Crab Cakes with Pommery Mustard Sauce 45
  Cracked Conch 31
  Curry Dipping Sauce 33
  Florida Ponzu Sauce 57
  Garlic & Beer Marinated Peel & Eat Shrimp 40
  Garlic Butter Sauce 40
  Grilled Avocados 55
  Hot Blue Crab Dip 47
  Key Lime Mustard Sauce for Stone Crabs 48
  Key Lime Wasabi Aioli 29
  Lobster Mango Guacamole 49
  Marinated Tempura Shrimp with Florida Ponzu Dipping Sauce 57
  Mignonette Sauce for Raw Oysters 43
  Pickled Vegetable Salsa 49
  Pimento Cheese 42
  Piña Colada Chicken Skewers 51
  Ponzu Sauce for Raw Oysters 43
  Preserved Key Limes 59
  Preserved Key Lime Vinaigrette 59
  Remoulade Sauce 37
  Rosemary & Garlic Grilled Shrimp 38
  Shrimp Cargot 39
  Shrimp Remoulade 37
  Tartar Sauce 48
  Tuna Poke 36
  Twice-Cooked Chipotle Barbecued Wings 53
  Wasabi-Mango Puree 41
  Yellowtail Snapper Ceviche 34

B

Baked Oysters Barrios 56
Ballyhoo's Coconut Milk Marinated Chicken 135
Ballyhoo's Jalapeño Cornbread 71
Ballyhoo's Pan Fried Hog Fish with Conch Salad Salsa 103
Banana Bread 159
Beal, Karen 54
Bill Baxter 32
Bill Wharton (The Sauce Boss) 120
Black Caesar 60
Blackened Shrimp Tacos with Chipotle Sour Cream and Orange Pico De Gallo 87
Blackwater Pasta 116
Blue Crab Soup 67
Bob Stoky Sr. 3, 46
Bouillabaisse 121
Bread
   Ballyhoo's Jalapeño Cornbread 71
   Banana Bread Recipe 159
   Luau Bread 72
   Mango Bread 72
   Pretzel Bread 78
Brunch & Breakfast
   Banana Bread 159
   Fresh Fruit with Florida Citrus Cream 160
   Garlic Cheese Grits Casserole 162
   Grits and Grunts 162
   Key Lime Hollandaise Sauce 161
   Lobster Benedict 161
   Sunshine French Toast 158
Butter Baked Lionfish with Fresh Vegetables 100
Butters
   Garlic Butter Sauce 40
   Key Lime Butter 97
   Orange Butter 158

C

Charbroiled Oysters 41
Chef Andre Mueller 32
Chef Salvador Barrios 56
Chicken 51, 53, 73, 90, 95, 97, 100, 116, 119, 120, 123, 124, 126, 128, 130, 131, 135, 138
Chicken & Yellow Rice 128
Chimichurri Sauce 130
Chipotle Barbecued Wings 53
Chipotle Barbecue Sauce 52
Chocolate Ganache 149

Chocolate-Orange Cuban Bread Pudding 154
Chocolate Pecan Pie 153
Churasco Steak with Chimichurri Sauce 130
Clam Chowder 66
Classic Key Lime Mojito 19
Cocktails
  21 Coconuts 15
  Classic Key Lime Mojito 19
  Coconut Margarita 21
  Flagler Express 13
  Grilled Pineapple Margarita 22
  Hemingway Cocktail 15
  Key Lime Martini 16
  Mango Mojito 19
  Organic Margarita 20
  Original Margarita 20
  Piña Colada 11
  Pomegranate Sangria 23
  Rum Runner 11
  Sea Salt 17
  Simple Syrup 14
  Spiced Hawaiian Punch 13
  Watermelon Mojito 18
  White Peach Sangria 23
Cocktail Sauce 29
Coconut Margarita 21
Coconut Telegraph 60
Conch 26, 27, 29, 30, 31, 33, 62, 63, 65, 70, 103, 126
Conch Chowder 63
Conch Chowder, Traditional 63
Conch Chowder, White 65
Conch Egg Rolls 27
Conch Fritters with Curry Dipping Sauce 33
Conch Republic 26
Conch Salad 30
Contents 5, 163
Corn 106
Corn Meal Fried Oysters with Mango Salsa 99
Cozumel Shrimp Cocktail 35
Crab Avocado Stack 79
Crab Cakes with Pommery Mustard Sauce 45
Cracked Conch 31
Craig Belcher 85
Crispy Onion Straws for Salads, Burgers and more 73
Cuban Style Shepherd's Pie 136
Cumin Encrusted Mahi Mahi Tacos 89
Curry Dipping Sauce 33

D

Darden, Mikey 4
Dedication 3
Deep 6 Marina 60
Desserts
  Chocolate-Orange Cuban Bread Pudding 154
  Chocolate Pecan Pie 153
  Florida Strawberry & Peach "Melba" 151
  Key Lime Baked Alaska 150
  Key Lime Cake 156
  Key Lime Fudge 145
  Key Lime Raspberry Squares 147
  Mango Pie 146
  Profiteroles 148
  Roasted Banana and Toffee Trifle 155
  Strawberry Bruschetta on Raisin Bread Toast 152
  Sundowners' World-Famous Key Lime Pie 142
Dressings
  Mango Citrus Vinaigrette Dressing 76
  Mangrove Honey-Lime Vinaigrette Dressing 75
  Orange Dill Ranch Dressing 75
  Oriental Dressing 76
  Remoulade Dressing 79
  Shoyu Salad Dressing 81

E

Entrees 127
  Amaretto Mashed Sweet Potatoes with Marshmallows 107
  Ballyhoo's Coconut Milk Marinated Chicken 135
  Ballyhoo's Pan Fried Hog Fish with Conch Salad Salsa 103
  Blackened Shrimp Tacos with Chipotle Sour Cream and Orange Pico De Gallo 87
  Blackwater Pasta 116
  Bouillabaisse 121
  Butter Baked Lionfish with Fresh Vegetables 100
  Chicken & Yellow Rice 128
  Chimichurri Sauce 130
  Churasco Steak with Chimichurri Sauce 130
  Corn Meal Fried Oysters with Mango Salsa 99
  Cuban Style Shepherd's Pie 136
  Cumin Encrusted Mahi Mahi Tacos 89
  Florida Orange Glaze 127
  Florida Orange Glazed Chicken with Cilantro 126
  Fried Ballyhoo 102
  Ginger Grilled Tuna with Pineapple Ponzu 109
  Grilled Chicken Tacos with Avocado and Corn Salsa 95
  Grilled Corn with Tomatoes, Roasted Jalapeños, and Fresh Cilantro 106
  Grilled Mahi Tacos with Citrus Pico de Gallo and Fresh Summer Corn 93

Grilled Mango Chicken Tacos with Avocado and Queso Fresco 90
Grouper Martinique with Tomato Basil Concasse and Bananas 112
Island Style Fish Poached in Coconut Milk 110
Key Lime Butter 97
Key West Pink Shrimp au Gratin 129
Key West Pink Shrimp, Chicken and Sausage Gumbo 119
Lightly Blackened Yellowtail Snapper with Mango Salsa 108
Loaded Paella 123
Lobster Fajitas 91
Lobster Pot Pie 92
Lobster Tacos with Cabbage Slaw and Avocado Cream 96
Mango Salsa 99
Mangrove Honey & Chipotle Glazed Rib Eye 134
Marinated Key Lime Turkey 138
Mojo Mahi Bites 115
Mojo Marinade 104
Mojo Marinated Whole Fried Yellowtail Snapper 105
Onion Encrusted Lobster with Key Lime Butter 97
Original Harvey's Fish Sandwich 85
Palomilla Steak 132
Picadillo with Sweet Corn Polenta Mashed Potatoes "Cuban Style Shepherd's Pie" 136
Pineapple Ponzu Sauce 109
Roasted Tomato Salsa 98
Seared Scallops with White Beans and Pancetta 125
Simple Grilled Fish with Yellow Rice and Peas 101
Soft Corn Taco Shells 94
Sticky Coconut Rice 111
Sundowners' Key Lime Seafood 118
Sundowners' Tartar Sauce 98
Sweet Corn Polenta Mashed Potatoes 137
Swordfish Mediterranean 113
Tamarind-Rubbed Pork Tenderloin 131
Tomato Basil Concasse 112
Tuna Burger 86

F

Fajitas
  Lobster Fajitas 91
Feeding the Tarpon 44
Flagler Express 13
Flagler's Folly 12
Florida Orange Glaze 127
Florida Orange Glazed Chicken with Cilantro 126
Florida Ponzu Sauce 57
Florida Strawberry & Peach "Melba" 151
Fresh Fruit with Florida Citrus Cream 160
Fried Ballyhoo 102

G

Garlic & Beer Marinated Peel & Eat Shrimp 40
Garlic Butter Sauce 40
Garlic Cheese Grits Casserole 162
Garlic Croutons 69
Ginger Grilled Tuna with Pineapple Ponzu 109
Glazes
   Florida Orange Glaze 127
   Key Lime Glaze 156
   Mangrove Honey & Chipotle Glaze 134
Grilled Avocados 55
Grilled Chicken Tacos with Avocado and Corn Salsa 95
Grilled Corn with Tomatoes, Roasted Jalapeños, and Fresh Cilantro 106
Grilled Mahi Tacos with Citrus Pico de Gallo and Fresh Summer Corn 93
Grilled Mango Chicken Tacos with Avocado and Queso Fresco 90
Grilled Pineapple Margarita 22
Grits and Grunts 162
Grouper 109, 112
Grouper Martinique with Tomato Basil Concasse and Bananas 112
Grunts 162
Guy, Melody 107

H

Harvey Rosen 85
Hemingway 15
Hemingway Cocktail 15
History of Marker 88 32
History of the Conch Republic 26
History of the Rum Runner 10
Hog Fish 103
Holiday Isle Resort's Tiki Bar 10
Honorary Conchs 62
Hot Blue Crab Dip 47
How Sundowners Began 46
Hurricane Dipping Oil 68

I

Island Style Fish Poached in Coconut Milk 110

J

Jimmy Buffett 15, 21

K

Key Lime Baked Alaska 150
Key Lime Butter 97
Key Lime Cake 156

Key Lime Cream 149
Key Lime Fudge 145
Key Lime Hollandaise Sauce 161
Key Lime Martini 16
Key Lime Mustard Sauce for Stone Crabs 48
Key Lime Pie 16, 60, 142, 143, 150, 156
Key Lime Raspberry Squares 147
Key Lime Wasabi Aioli 29
Key West Pink Shrimp au Gratin 129
Key West Pink Shrimp, Chicken and Sausage Gumbo 119

L

Lewis, Andrew 114
Lightly Blackened Yellowtail Snapper with Mango Salsa 108
Lionfish 100
Loaded Paella 123
Lobster 49, 91, 92, 96, 97, 104, 161
Lobster Benedict 161
Lobster Fajitas 91
Lobster Mango Guacamole 49
Lobster Pot Pie 92
Lobster Tacos with Cabbage Slaw and Avocado Cream 96
Luau Bread 72

M

Mahi 89, 93, 115
Mango Bread 72
Mango Citrus Vinaigrette Dressing 76
Mango Mojito 19
Mango Pie 146
Mangos 14
Mango Salsa 99
Mangrove Honey & Chipotle Glazed Rib Eye 134
Mangrove Honey-Lime Vinaigrette Dressing 75
Mangroves of Key Largo 74
Margaritas
  Coconut Margarita 21
  Grilled Pineapple Margarita 22
  Original Margarita 20
Marinades
  Garlic & Beer Marinade 40
  Key Lime, Garlic, Wine & Olive Oil Marinade 38
  Mojo Marinade 104, 115
Marinated Key Lime Turkey 138
Marinated Tempura Shrimp with Florida Ponzu Dipping Sauce 57
Mignonette Sauce for Raw Oysters 43

Mojito 17
   Classic Key Lime Mojito 19
   Mango Mojito 19
   Watermelon Mojito 18
Mojo Mahi Bites 115
Mojo Marinade 104, 115
Mojo Marinated Whole Fried Yellowtail Snapper 105

O

Onion Encrusted Lobster with Key Lime Butter 97
Orange Butter 158
Orange Dill Ranch Dressing 75
Organic Margarita 20
Oriental Dressing 76
Original Harvey's Fish Sandwich 85
Original Margarita 20
Overseas Highway 12
Oysters 41, 43, 56, 99

P

Paella 123
Palomilla Steak 132
Paradise... Legal or Illegal? 60
Picadillo with Sweet Corn Polenta Mashed Potatoes "Cuban Style Shepherd's Pie" 136
Pickled Vegetable Salsa 49
Pimento Cheese 42
Piña Colada 11
Piña Colada Chicken Skewers 51
Pineapple Cole Slaw 77
Pineapple Plantations - Plantation Key 54
Pineapple Ponzu Sauce 109
Plantation Key 54
Pomegranate Sangria 23
Pommery Mustard Sauce 45
Ponzu 43, 57, 109
Ponzu Sauce for Raw Oysters 43
Preserved Key Limes 59
Preserved Key Lime Vinaigrette 59
Pretzel Bread 78
Profiteroles 148

R

Remoulade Dressing 79
Remoulade Sauce 37
Roasted Banana and Toffee Trifle 155
Roasted Tomato Salsa 98
Romano, Kathy 120

Rosemary & Garlic Grilled Shrimp 38
Rum Runner 11

S

Salsa 49, 95, 98, 99, 103, 108
Salvador Barrios 56
Sandwiches
  Original Harvey's Fish Sandwich 85
  Tuna Burger 86
Sangria
  Pomegranate Sangria 23
  White Peach Sangria 23
Saino, Helen 162
Sauce Boss 120
Sauces
  Chimichurri Sauce 130
  Chipotle Barbecue Sauce 52
  Cocktail Sauce 29
  Curry Dipping Sauce 33
  Florida Orange Glaze 127
  Florida Ponzu Sauce 57
  Garlic Butter Sauce 40
  Key Lime Butter 97
  Key Lime Hollandaise Sauce 161
  Pineapple Ponzu Sauce 109
  Pommery Mustard Sauce 45
  Ponzu Sauce for Raw Oysters 43
  Remoulade Sauce 37
  Sundowners' Tartar Sauce 98
  Tartar Sauce 48
  Thai Peanut Sauce 77
  Tomato Basil Concasse 112
  Wasabi-Mango Puree 41
Scallops 125
Scott Stoky 3, 28
Seared Scallops with White Beans and Pancetta 125
Sea Salt 17
Seasoned Oyster Crackers 68
Shoyu Salad Dressing 81
Shrimp 27, 29, 33, 35, 37, 38, 39, 40, 52, 57, 87, 97, 116, 118, 119, 120, 121, 123, 124, 129
Shrimp Cargot 39
Shrimp Remoulade 37
Simple Grilled Fish with Yellow Rice and Peas 101
Simple Syrup 14
Snapper 34, 105, 108
Soft Corn Taco Shells 94

Soups & Salads
- Ballyhoo's Jalapeño Cornbread 71
- Blue Crab Soup 67
- Bouillabaisse 121
- Clam Chowder 66
- Crab Avocado Stack 79
- Crispy Onion Straws for Salads, Burgers and more 73
- Garlic Croutons 69
- Hurricane Dipping Oil 68
- Key West Pink Shrimp, Chicken and Sausage Gumbo 119
- Luau Bread 72
- Mango Bread 72
- Mango Citrus Vinaigrette Dressing 76
- Mangrove Honey-Lime Vinaigrette Dressing 75
- Orange Dill Ranch Dressing 75
- Oriental Dressing 76
- Pineapple Cole Slaw 77
- Pretzel Bread 78
- Remoulade Dressing 79
- Seasoned Oyster Crackers 68
- Shoyu Salad Dressing 81
- Spiced Pale Dry Sherry 69
- Sundowners' Black Caesar's Blackening Spice 73
- Thai Peanut Sauce 77
- Traditional Conch Chowder 63
- White Conch Chowder 65

Spiced Hawaiian Punch 13
Spiced Pale Dry Sherry 69
Square Grouper 60
Steak 130, 132
Sticky Coconut Rice 111
Stoky, Ruthie 3
Stories
- All about Conchs! 62
- Feeding the Tarpon 44
- Flagler's Folly 12
- History of Marker 88 32
- History of the Conch Republic 26
- History of the Rum Runner 10
- Holiday Isle Resort's Tiki Bar 10
- Honorary Conchs 62
- How Sundowners Began 46
- Mangos 14
- Mangroves of Key Largo 74
- Mojito 17
- Pain in the Ass (cocktail) 10
- Paradise... Legal or Illegal? 60

Piña Colada 10
Pineapple Plantations - Plantation Key 54
Rum Runner 10
Scott Stoky, Junior Master Angler 28
Welcome 7
Why is Ballyhoo's Legendary? 70
World Famous Rum Runner 10
Strawberry Bruschetta on Raisin Bread Toast 152
Sundowners' Black Caesar's Blackening Spice 37, 40, 45, 73, 87, 92, 93, 97, 108, 109, 119, 129
Sundowners' Key Lime Seafood 118
Sundowners' Tartar Sauce 98
Sundowners' World-Famous Key Lime Pie 142
Sunshine French Toast 158
Sweet Corn Polenta Mashed Potatoes 137
Sweet Potatoes 107
Swordfish 113
Swordfish Mediterranean 113

T

Tacos
   Blackened Shrimp Tacos with Chipotle Sour Cream and Orange Pico De Gallo 87
   Cumin Encrusted Mahi Mahi Tacos 89
   Grilled Chicken Tacos with Avocado and Corn Salsa 95
   Grilled Mahi Tacos with Citrus Pico de Gallo and Fresh Summer Corn 93
   Grilled Mango Chicken Tacos with Avocado and Queso Fresco 90
   Lobster Tacos with Cabbage Slaw and Avocado Cream 96
   Soft Corn Taco Shells 94
Tamarind Rub 131
Tamarind-Rubbed Pork Tenderloin 131
Tartar Sauce 48
Thai Peanut Sauce 77
Tiki John Ebert 10, 11
Tomato Basil Concasse 112
Traditional Conch Chowder 63
Tuna 36, 76, 86, 109
Tuna Burger 86
Tuna Poke 36
Turkey 138, 139
Twenty-One Coconuts 15
Twice-Cooked Chipotle Barbecued Wings 53

W

Wasabi-Mango Puree 41
Watermelon Mojito 18
Welcome 7
White, Paul 4, 162

White Peach Sangria 23
Why is Ballyhoo's Legendary? 70
World Famous Rum Runner 10

Y

Yellowtail 34, 105, 108
Yellowtail Snapper Ceviche 34

Index | 175